Bolivia, Paraguay and Brazil Fires burning north of the Paraguay River near Puerto Busch. Recently burned areas appear black. This year saw a surge in Amazon rainforest wildfires, prompting widespread international concern, as they capture much of the Earth's carbon dioxide. Photo: NASA Earth Observatory images by Joshua Stevens, using Landsat data from the US Geological Survey

Paris, France People cool off in and around a large water pool at Trocadero, across the Seine from the Eiffel Tower. During a Europe-wide heatwave last summer, the temperature in the city reached 42ºC – a high for the year that broke the previous record of 40.4ºC, set in July 1947. Five people died from heatstroke. Photo: Getty

Ladbroke Hill, UK Plastic casings containing thousands of dead saplings planted to replace trees that will be cut down to make way for HS2. As many as 85% of the 35,000 trees planted died during the drought in 2018 – HS2 decided not to water them, as it was cheaper and "more ethical" to replace them instead. Photo: @StopHS2

Addis Ababa, Ethiopia A young Ethiopian girl takes part in a national tree-planting drive. The country plans to plant four billion trees by the end of October, as part of a global movement to fight climate change and protect resources by restoring forests. Ethiopia said it had planted nearly three billion trees since May. Photo: Getty

London, UK Extinction Rebellion erected a 'Leonardo Da Vinci bridge' in London, designed to collapse when a piece of wood is removed, thus becoming a road block. Two weeks of protests in major cities around the world occupied public space to highlight governments' perceived lack of action against climate change. Photo: Guilhem Baker

Dublin Castle, Ireland EcoLogicStudio architects Marco Poletto and Claudia Pasquero's Photo.Synth.Etica enables microalgal cultures to feed off sunlight, releasing oxygen. Two square metres can absorb the same amount of CO_2 that a mature tree can, so this 224 square metre installation could do the same work as a small park. Photo: NAARO

Milan, Italy Designed by famous Italian architect Pietro Lingeri in the 1950s for McLaren, the Sempione Green Garage has been repurposed by architecture studio Labics to create a nursery, kindergarten and sports centre with three swimming pools – a spectacular example of re-use. Three bridges are suspended between the arches to form classrooms. Photos: Delfino Sisto Legnani and Marco Cappelletti

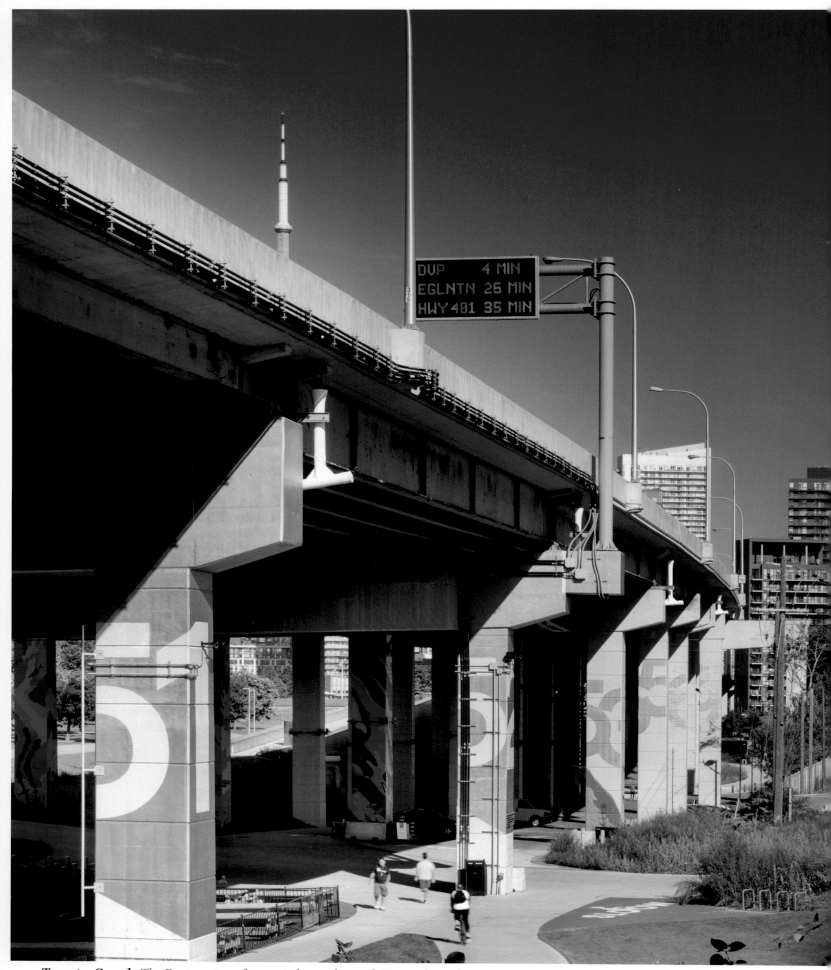

Toronto, Canada The Bentway transforms 1.75km underneath Toronto's Gardiner Expressway into a new green corridor for the city's population. It also offers year-round activities and events, and features an ice-skating trail. Photos (clockwise from above): Nic Lehoux, Andrew Williamson and Denise Militzer

Toronto, Canada Running underneath the Gardiner Expressway, The Bentway functions as walking and cycling infrastructure and cultural venue with an annual programme of events and activities. The Museum of the Moon in Strachan Gate is a seven-metre wide touring sculpture by UK artist Luke Jerram. Photo: Nicola Betts

Toronto, Canada The first phase of The Bentway knits together seven local neighbourhoods, home to more than 70,000 residents, and connects through to Lake Ontario and the Fort York National Historic Site. Toronto's waterfront was cut off by the motorway in the 1960s.
Photo: Nic Lehoux

the developer resilience

Placetest: MediaCityUK in Manchester, p104

Glasgow's plan for its high streets, p80

Making music in the gaps, p94

Tottenham is undergoing rapid development change, p48

Visiting co-housing project Marmalade Lane, p66

Miami's resilient city project, p186

places

research

Placetest: Festival of Place, p164

festival of place

It is almost one year since we launched *The Developer* My ambition in launching this title, then and now, writes editor-in-chief Christine Murray, is to bring together developers, government, designers, investors and other makers of place, to serve them with thought-provoking content and enable conversations through the Festival of Place, to help us shape better cities

There are times when serving the industry and sparking conversation means sharing hard truths. That is why in this edition we highlight the industry's negative contribution to air pollution, mental health, biodiversity and flood risk and what to do about it.

That is also what led me to investigate the use of pesticides in our cities and public spaces, which uncovered that 98% of councils use weedkillers containing glyphosate, applying it to housing estates, playgrounds, pavements and public spaces.

That story, nominated for Scoop of the Year at the IBP awards, fundamentally questions our design approach to public space. If we need to spray our urban realm with a suspected carcinogen for maintenance, we are doing something wrong.

When the story broke online it was illustrated with the spraying of tree pits on the King's Crescent Estate. Hackney's award-winning mixed-tenure housing development designed by Karakusevic Carson gets a lot of things right, but not this.

The fact that Milton Keynes is the biggest user of glyphosate herbicide is proof positive that we need to rethink the Modernist aesthetic that has captured our imagination for so long. The design of public space is neither rational, nor functional, if it requires the widespread use of poison to maintain it. Indeed, these barren townscapes are a failure – wasting water and failing to support the health of humans, not to mention animals, birds and bugs.

No wonder the only thriving urban species are cockroaches, rats and pigeons.

And yet, architects still proudly describe themselves as Modernists, churning out £123bn-worth of masterplans across the UK – a plague of concrete-scapes with LED-lit fountains, shared-surface streets and spongy playgrounds, with sculptures perched on patches of plastic grass. Pesticides torture rebel weeds pushing through the cracks as nature fights back. Meanwhile rainwater runs off into Victorian fatberg-ridden sewers without replenishing precious aquifers, or washes pollution into streams and reservoirs of drinking water.

Windswept plazas are just one example of how we have been so focused on adding value to real estate that we have, paradoxically, left land poorer, stripping this shared asset. If scientists have woken up to the power of the human microbiome, we are still eradicating the good bacteria of our cities. The irony is that many of these beautification projects are sculpted by professionals who commute into town from greener pastures, for some reason believing city dwellers deserve the plastic-covered sofa equivalent to the countryside – the wipe-clean city.

Christine Murray. Photo: Anthony Coleman

What's wrong with a little mud? How did we move so far away from the English landscape garden, with its wabi-sabi elegance, wafting willow trees and Monet-ready ponds? There is some evidence the tide is turning, not led by any design trend (although Piet Oudolf's High Line has proved influential), but by necessity: new planning hurdles are pushing biodiversity net gain and sustainable urban drainage to mitigate the heat island effect, wildlife loss and rising flood and drought risk.

As Dirk van Peijpe says in this edition, "we need to move from a drainage city to a sponge city" and fundamentally rethink our relationship to the elements – stop designing out nature, and design with it. The work of professionals such as Kevin Barton at Robert Bray Associates, are leading the way in the UK towards hairier, more resilient, wild-yet-urban places. But before you outsource this all to your landscape architect, read this: real estate needs a deeper mindset shift. As placemakers, we need to disrupt the very way we approach the design and development of our cities.

For too long, redevelopment has been a colonial act. We disperse citizens through compulsory purchase or decanting, making false promises with unrealistic CGIs. We speak of places being "regenerated" as though they are degenerate, adopting the language of slum clearance and 'savages'. We approach design and feasibility studies based on extracting maximum value from the land, squeezing in the most flats.

We claim to be creating communities even as we cleave them apart into poor cores and segregated playgrounds. Finally, we market the property to new settlers: inviting

gentrifiers to colonise the neighbourhood.

The approach has, in many cases, won investment and turned a profit, yet the trustworthiness and reputation of developers among the public has fallen to new and profound lows. As for making a positive social impact, even the mammoth east London project for a lasting Olympic legacy has, on the whole, failed to improve the lot of its citizens. The London Assembly 2017 report, *Relighting the Torch: Securing the Olympic Legacy,* found that after construction jobs faded away, the gap in the median earnings for full-time workers living in the area actually worsened from 2009 levels, as well as rates of childhood obesity, adult activity levels and overcrowding.

Now, government data on the Indices of Deprivation 2019 released in September reveals, while overall London is less deprived than in 2015, "barriers to housing and services" – which measures homelessness, housing affordability, distance to essential services and overcrowding – is worse. And nearly all of Olympic-borough Newham falls into the most deprived 5% in England. A further black mark on this industry: housing deprivation is the only one of all seven indices that has declined.

Depressing facts, but don't give up now. Here lies opportunity: UK cities are still growing and Manchester and Liverpool are well placed to learn from London's failures. Modernist infrastructure is undergoing renewal and we have the imperative to do things differently. The market is also moving at a pace where we can take time to re-educate ourselves and think before we act.

We must abandon the colonial language of so-called regeneration, reject failed Modernist doctrines and instead focus on enabling, listening, sharing and supporting our citizens – moving from extraction to provision. We have to stop the 'engagement' of communities in battle, and build with them, and learn from the hopeful stories of places such as Marmalade Lane.

As we reimagine the future city, we must develop a radical new urban aesthetic supported by the new climate planning imperatives to de-pave and re-wild. Citizens have already embraced weeds as wildflowers. What next? What are your blockers? Let's move them out of the way, together.

The Developer has been shortlisted in the IBP awards for Editorial Brand of the Year, Scoop of the Year and Event of the Year for Festival of Place

Find out more
https://data.london.gov.uk/blog/indices-of-deprivation-2019-initial-analysis/

Designed in the early '70s, Milton Keynes' Modernist public spaces do not differ wildly from many projects designed today. Pictured here in 2010, architecture critic Owen Hatherley describes this 'new town' as the "doomed apotheosis of the fossil-fuel society". Photo: Getty

"London will flood and when it happens, it will be dramatic" A failure of the Thames Barrier is inevitable and will happen soon. Anna White looks at the challenges facing us and where true resilience lies

Following a violent storm that raged throughout the UK, France, Belgium, Holland and Germany in 1949, the Thames overflowed, flooding the Parliament and Westminster quays. Photo: Getty

Picture this: a fierce northerly wind whips up a storm surge in the narrow North Sea, battering the east coast of England. It funnels into the Thames Estuary and gathers pace towards London.

The rain is lashing down on the capital, the wind is raging, the tide high, the pressure low and the Thames Barrier shuts.

This precise swell of factors creates the perfect storm. Waterloo's Lower Marsh floods and waves penetrate Westminster. No amount of armed security guards or crash bollards can prevent this environmental attack on the heart of Britain's political establishment.

"The 500-year storm has become a one-in-20-year occurrence or even less. London will flood and when it happens, it will be dramatic," says Asif Din, sustainability director of global architectural firm Perkins+Will.

The combination of rising water levels and increasing frequency of catastrophic weather events means climate change can no longer be dismissed as a futuristic threat to communities, buildings and infrastructure.

"The short-term impacts are getting worse just as long-term change is taking hold – it is a double whammy," says Ian Allison, global head of climate resilience at engineering group Mott MacDonald. It is a "right-now problem".

Surely the Thames Barrier, which opened in 1982 and sits just east of the Isle of Dogs, will protect the Greater London floodplain against storm surges?

The iconic blockade, which shut only 10 times in its first decade, shut 74 times in the past decade to March this year. "A failure of the Thames Barrier is inevitable and, on current projections, will happen soon," says Din.

In the 1940s, a tidal surge of 3.66 metres was recorded in the Thames but hit at low tide, leaving the city unscathed. If it had coincided with the highest possible tide of the year, the waves would have increased to

According to an insider, climate change is no longer the elephant in the room at Lloyd's of London, the global insurance sector headquarters. The insurance broker told *The Developer*: 'Climate change is the topic of the moment in the corridors of Lloyd's of London. The industry is panicking about how to tackle it'

6.86 metres – just 14cm shy of the height of the Thames Barrier.

Given the effects of global warming since then, it is not hard to imagine London's last line of defence being overwhelmed in a worst-case scenario.

Architect Rory Bergin of HTA Design agrees: "Half of the South depends on the Thames Barrier – a breach really is the elephant in the room."

Most central London developments rely on the future implementation of Thames Estuary 2100 (TE2100), the Environment Agency's £300m tidal defence and flood risk programme of construction across the Thames Estuary.

According to an insider, climate change is no longer the elephant in the room at Lloyd's of London, the global insurance sector headquarters.

The insurance broker told *The Developer*: "Climate change is the topic of the moment in the corridors of Lloyd's of London. The industry is panicking about how to tackle it."

A recent report from the Urban Land Institute (ULI) summarises the scale and complexity of this right-now problem for the insurance industry.

"In the long run, the consequence of climate risks such as sea-level rises and extreme heat will increasingly highlight the vulnerability of individual assets, locations and entire metropolitan areas," it reads.

Real estate investors are fearful of insurance premiums being driven up as a result of climate change, but the cost of failing to insure is astronomical.

The repair bill after Hurricane Katrina, which hit the US and Caribbean in 2005, is estimated to be £83bn. In 2016, losses from natural disasters worldwide totalled £142bn, but only £39bn was covered by insurance,

according to insurance firm Munich Re.

In 2017, the year that Hurricanes Harvey and Maria hit the US and spin-off storms battered central and northern Europe, insurance companies paid out $135bn. That year, the actual damage done by storms and natural disasters in the US alone stood at $307bn.

The unpredictability of future weather patterns plays havoc with actuarial modelling, and therefore adds another layer of complexity for underwriters.

Insurance companies rely on historical loss records to guide underwriting and pricing. However, with the climate acting in a manner that is increasingly hard to predict, the historical data is losing its value.

According to the ULI report, a growing group of investors and investment managers are exploring new approaches to find better tools and common standards to help the industry get better at pricing in climate risk in the future.

These include mapping physical risk for current portfolios and potential acquisitions; incorporating climate risk into due diligence and other investment decision-making processes; incorporating additional physical adaptation and mitigation measures for assets at risk; exploring a variety of strategies to mitigate risk, including portfolio diversification and investing directly in the mitigation measures for specific assets; and engaging with policymakers on city-level resilience strategies, and supporting the investment by cities in mitigating the risk of all assets under their jurisdiction.

There is also a vital need for an interplay between the insurance industry, the government (setting building regulations) and the development community (adhering to the regulations).

A scheme that might be resilient now will not be constructed to withstand a storm surge of a magnitude possible in 30 years' time.

So who is ultimately responsible for a building or place that is doomed to fail?

Currently, it would fall to the homeowner and an individual's home insurance policy – which as yet might not account for the escalating magnitude of hurricanes, extreme precipitation, tornadoes, landslides, mudflows, drought, wildfires, heatwaves, flash floods and rising sea levels.

A spokesperson for Lloyd's of London skilfully puts the ball in the government's court: "Insurers provide insurance to properties that have been built in accordance with current government regulations.

"We... rely upon government and those with a more specialist building construction knowledge to provide the bulk of technical

An unusually long heatwave last summer turned parks and other grasslands into 'tinderboxes'. Photo: Getty

Torrential rain caused a flash flood in Wallington, Sutton, in 2016. Photo: Rex Features

Co-operative's Manchester HQ has a heat recovery system and 300,000 sq ft of exposed concrete that acts as a thermal sponge. Photo: Alamy

32

One Blackfriars is made from 5,476 sheets of curved glass and changes colour at different times of the day. Photo: Alamy

guidance to the government of the day to ensure dwellings are compliant with current regulations around life safety and construction regulations."

One global initiative is lobbying policymakers, insurers and investors to take responsibility and ensure infrastructure is both financially and physically resilient.

The United Nations-affiliated task force, icebreakerone.org, is calling for a "new class of insurance combined with market standard risk transparency... and an open environment risk standard".

Rather than wait for new building standards to be formalised, construction techniques must change now. "We can adapt to long-term incremental climate change but it is the 'what if', one-off catastrophic event that we have to plan for in our built environment," says Din.

Urban areas are hotter than their rural surroundings. Materials such as concrete and glass, combined with a high level of movement from cars and motorbikes, public transport and even the motion of people, heat up the ground and air during the day while towers block cooling breezes.

Buildings must be designed to reduce the amount of solar input with proper shading and passive ventilation. They also need to be comfortable on the inside, Din explains.

Overheating buildings are a public health crisis in the making. In the wake of Hurricane Katrina, air conditioning failed and temperatures soared. The city's hospital staff had to smash sealed windows in order to let air into the building. "Patients were trapped in an overheating glass box," Din says.

The vase-like new tower in Southwark, One Blackfriars, is made from 5,476 sheets of curved glass and sculpted to catch and reflect the light, changing colour at different times of the day. One architect describes it as "a building designed to overheat".

But Rachel Haugh of SimpsonHaugh, the firm which designed the building, says: "One Blackfriars is often described as an all-glass building but this is a common misreading. Between two independent skins is a winter

Barking Riverside is being built at a far higher level than planned, with more flood defences

> Some developers are still too focused on a building's good looks rather than its good performance. Not everything has to be wall-to-wall glass. It's about getting the ratio of wall to window right

garden. In winter, the louvres on the outer skin close, offering an 'overcoat' of warm air to the inner building. In summer, louvres open, allowing the trapped heat to dissipate."

One Blackfriars is unique as far as glass towers go, having been designed to an impressive Code for Sustainable Homes Level 4 standard. Its retail provision is rated BREEAM Very Good, with its hotel achieving BREEAM Excellent. The tower also features air-source heat pumps and rainwater tanks to reduce the chance of flash flooding.

Din says: "The days of the all-glass tower are numbered." However, he does cite "fritting" as a useful technique when constructing resilient buildings. This is the addition of a porous glass sublayer that reduces the amount of solar energy.

The housebuilding industry is trapped in a vicious circle. In an escalating housing supply crisis and with limited space on which to build, the only way is up.

But Bob Weston, founder and chair of Weston Homes, argues that tall towers are prone to overheating as they have more surface area to absorb sunlight.

"Our understanding of the effects of weather on buildings has come on leaps and bounds in the past five years," says Bergin of HTA. "However, some developers are still too focused on a building's good looks rather than its good performance. Not everything has to be wall-to-wall glass. It's about getting the ratio of wall to window right."

Air conditioning intensifies the problem, taking heat from inside and moving it outside, warming the external temperature and increasing the temperature of the urban heat island – perpetuating the need for more air con. "Unprotected glass buildings that need to be artificially cooled is a poor strategy," Bergin says.

He favours a simple approach: keep the heat out by making the windows the right size for the amount of daylight needed with shading and shutters instead. "We should look to our continental neighbours. External shutters are the normal fabric of their residential buildings, and are left closed during the day," he says.

A westerly-facing apartment will get a lot of sun, therefore it should be designed to have dual-aspect windows so that the resident can get a breeze flowing through.

Construction group Tide is building a 550-apartment development at 101 George Street in Croydon. On completion, it will comprise two of the world's tallest modular towers, part-built in a factory and put together on site, at 44 and 38 floors.

The building is clad in green perforated terracotta panels that let in light but keep the heat out, therefore creating thermal stability. Each flat will have mechanical ventilation – a high-tech fan that whirrs away silently, bringing fresh air in and expelling out stale air. The outgoing air heats the incoming air, keeping bills low.

One Angel Square, the Co-operative's headquarters in Manchester, was awarded BREEAM certification in 2013. The building has a heat recovery system to collect and recycle heat waste and 300,000 sq ft of exposed concrete that acts as a thermal sponge.

Then, there is the question of whole-life carbon, which includes not only the energy performance of the building after completion, but the emissions created by construction and in the making of its building materials such as brick, glass, steel and concrete – the worst offenders.

According to Steve Webb, director of Webb Yates Engineers, the best low-carbon cladding material in this post-Grenfell epoch is very thin metal or stone, which require less processing and are structurally sound; stone, unlike brick, does not require firing. As for wood and cross-laminated timber, Webb says: "There are real fire engineering challenges and rotting, but these issues need to be solved. The solution is not the abandonment of timber."

"We've only got one generation of buildings to get this right," says Basil Demeroutis, sustainability investor at the fund FORE.

Transport infrastructure is vulnerable, too. Even a slight increase in temperature can buckle train tracks, meaning rail operators have to apply speed limits during a heatwave, and hot tracks mean overnight maintenance cannot be carried out. As heavy rain and high winds result in landslides and fallen trees on railways, the dial moves from inconvenient to dangerous.

Construction for climate change is not just about future-proofing individual structures. True resilience lies in the holistic masterplanning of entire schemes and towns.

The space in between is as important as the buildings. A business district comprising tall towers must be designed so that high winds do not get trapped between buildings and, forced to find a way out, create powerful wind tunnels at ground level. It's also about better planning. Heron Tower in the City has PV solar panels on one facade to harness solar energy. That side is now overshadowed by newer buildings. There is no point having an award-winning, resilient building that is not in a resilient area, explains Mott MacDonald's Allison. "I've seen back-up flood barriers and back-up power sources that cannot be accessed in a storm."

Adaptability, not strength, is key in designing for an unstable atmospheric future. "Sacrificial car parks should be designed at basement level. Through good communication the residents know to move their cars in advance, the basement is allowed to flood and after it recedes can be cleaned and put back into use. It's all about flexibility," he adds.

Disaster relief centres should be ready to use at any time and always accessible. Power sub-stations must not be built in the basement or on the ground floor and the materials on those lower levels must be robust and easily cleaned after the event. "It's all about how quickly these sites and their communities can bounce back," says Din.

Long-term regeneration schemes can take 30 to 50 years from planning to completion, outlasting many a property or economic cycle. The Earth's temperature and water levels may even go up faster than the next penthouse or public viewing gallery, and initial plans can become outdated before the first shovels cut into the ground. The UN's latest climate report states that one-in-100-year events will happen annually by 2050.

Barking Riverside is being built at a far higher level than original proposals set out. "From a climate change adaption point of view, a major part of our approach has been to build resilience into our water management systems. We are raising and improving the flood defences along our 2km stretch of the River Thames to address the worst climate-change scenarios," says Sarah Coutts, head of planning and design of the 443-acre, 11,000-home mini-town.

More than 1,000,000m³ of soil was used to raise the development platform above flood level from the Thames and local tributaries, and the drainage strategy incorporates living roofs, permeable paving rain gardens and landscaped ponds.

"This creates sheltered micro-climates for wildlife and helps to reduce the effects of the urban heat island," Coutts adds.

The development company behind the conversion of Battersea Power Station is "refurbishing and raising river walls" to protect against flooding, and using green and

Kingston flooded in 1976, when a severe drought was followed by twice the average rainfall. Photo: Rex Features

brown roofs for storm-water attenuation.

The 'Sponge City' project in Glasgow is the creation of Europe's first smart canal. Sensor and predictive weather technology will provide an early warning of wet weather, before moving excess rainfall from residential and business areas (via urban drainage ponds to a network of granite channels) into the canal where water levels will have been lowered by as much as 10cm. This will create extra capacity for floodwater – the equivalent of 22 Olympic swimming pools. In turn this will open up 270 acres of underused space to the north of the city for regeneration, paving the way for the delivery of 3,000 new homes.

"By unlocking the inherent value of Glasgow's canal and diversifying the asset, we are ensuring it continues to deliver for local people 250 years after it was first built... Not only will it reduce the flood risk impact of climate change but it will act as a catalyst for new investment, jobs, homes and businesses," says Catherine Topley, chief executive of Scottish Canals.

It is not just the physical process of building that can crawl – the UK's rigid planning system also lags behind today's science.

"We won work on a site three times over a 12-year period," says Bergin. "The first two times, the site was handed back due to financial difficulties and by the third time, the flooding advice was dangerously out of date." He adds: "The UK governance and planning systems are very slow to react – it takes five years to agree a local plan, for example."

The large public-listed developers will have to start reporting on their environmental as well as financial performance due to pressure from investors

and out of reputational concern. But Allison worries that the private builders will only be obliged to meet anachronistic building regulations. The regulatory framework struggles to keep up with 'the now' and yet climate change scientists are planning and modelling for the next 30 to 80 years.

Those developers who wish to build sustainable schemes that can withstand extreme weather events employ architects and consultants to generate different weather scenarios for 100 years from now. Clearly there is a cost to this level of expertise.

Demeroutis believes there are good returns to be made from sustainable buildings: "Private capital is taking responsibility more seriously," he says. "They will no longer fund greenwashing."

The UK's Committee on Climate Change released a new report and new zero-emissions target for the UK in the spring. Britain is to be net zero greenhouse gases by 2050, in line with the United Nations' Sustainable Development Goals.

The pressure is not only top down but homeowners should vote with their wallets, too. Becky Fatemi, founder of property firm Rokstone, believes future-proofed homes will appeal to the next generation of first-time buyers who have eco-anxiety and awareness.

"One of the best-selling apartment blocks in London has been the Manhattan Loft Gardens in east London's Stratford, due to its three green sky gardens," she says.

So what of London's inevitable future flood? The Environment Agency will review its TE2100 plans next year. The entire development community must, for evermore, build for a breach.

The Thames flooded Chiswick Mall, London, in February 2016, after high tide reached 5.4 metres. Photo: Getty

Policemen rescuing residents of Clapton, London, in 1947 after the River Lea burst its banks. Photo: Getty

Portsmouth's once-in-a-generation community

There is a reason that groundbreaking plans for Tipner West are receiving national interest, following the recent launch to the industry – the dynamic project team has an innovative and forward-thinking approach that is causing excitement and acclaim

Tipner West is a 140-acre strategic, visual and economic gateway to Portsmouth

Tipner West is a unique development site where land meets sea. Surrounded by water yet directly connected to the M275, it is an iconic gateway that will enable generations of people to come to experience and understand the city of Portsmouth.

It therefore has a significant responsibility – to anticipate and answer the future needs of the city and its people.

Natascha McIntyre Hall, assistant director of regeneration at Portsmouth City Council, says: "At Tipner West, we have the chance to look beyond the horizon and pioneer a new way of living and working that is dedicated to the long-term flourishing of communities and the world we share."

Plans for Tipner West have recently taken an exciting leap forward. Following careful consideration, the project team at Portsmouth City Council devised a concept with architect Gensler that focuses on four important benefits of this exciting opportunity.

The case for a marine employment hub at Tipner West is crystal clear. The combination of deep water, excellent transport access and strategic position in the Solent marks it out as the industry's favoured spot to support critical growth for Portsmouth.

"We have the opportunity to directly influence and overcome some of the biggest issues facing modern cities. Tipner West will show a different way of creating new places"

A one million square foot marine employment campus will ensure the UK's position as a leader in the industry. Innovation is critical not only to secure national dominance in this sector but also to originate solutions in a changing world. Complete with R&D labs and makerspaces, Tipner West will kick-start, nurture and grow businesses, providing new jobs, skills and education opportunities, and economic resilience for Portsmouth.

Our homes, both the locations and the physical buildings themselves, influence almost every aspect of our lives, health and well-being. People are thinking hard about the environment in which they want to live and the impact their homes have on the world and other people – the next generation of people looking for homes want to live healthily, happily and ethically.

Tipner West will provide more than 4,000 new homes, which is roughly a quarter of Portsmouth's 2036 goal. However, these will not just be any homes. They will offer people ways to live sustainably, from construction methods to clean energy, all within the nature and beauty of the harbour. And they will be homes the people of Portsmouth, as well as the 41,000 highly-skilled workers who come into the city every day, can afford.

A sense of community is a modern imperative. We have a responsibility to

Key statistics
140 acres: Size of the development
4,000+: New homes that will be built
1 million square feet: Size of the marine employment campus
2,250 metres: Length of the waterfront

Launching to the industry

Above: CGI model of the Tipner West site

counteract loneliness and anxiety by helping people to feel connected and empowered, and to have a sense of belonging. People will be connected to each other by public gardens, the water and pedestrianised squares for eating and dining. This is an opportunity to lead nationally by creating connected and caring new communities.

Meanwhile, technology is providing tantalising solutions to our petrol addiction and cities are turning streets into playgrounds. That is why Tipner West will be designed for a future without cars and kerbs. An underground, centralised hub will not only allow for smart services, such as pneumatic waste collection, but also provide a car park large enough to conceal cars from everyday life.

Tipner West will be a new benchmark in people-based design, a development that will benefit everyone – completely accessible, safe, smart and beautifully designed.

Natascha McIntyre Hall says: "This is Portsmouth's time and Tipner West is

flying the flag for a progressive Portsmouth. We need to build on our growing reputation for leisure and capitalise on our highly skilled workforce. We require places for experimentation, to try new ways of living and working. We have the capability and spirit of adventure to achieve great advances."

Megan Carter, Portsmouth City Council's senior project manager, continues: "Tipner West will be a destination for leisure and a beacon for Portsmouth on the international stage. We have the opportunity to directly influence and overcome some of the biggest issues facing modern cities.

"Tipner West will show a different way of creating new places – places that thrive equally as drivers of economic success and powerful centres of societal good."

Tipner West really is a once-in-a-generation opportunity.

Portsmouth City Council is working alongside Savills, Gensler, Marina Projects, WSP and ECD Architects

Find out more at
tipnerwest.portsmouth.gov.uk

Please contact Megan Carter, senior project manager, on
02392 834723 or tipnerwest@
portsmouthcc.gov.uk

Below: Presenting Tipner West

Exclusive: 98% of councils use weedkiller linked to cancer in public spaces

The Developer's investigation reveals widespread use of the pesticide glyphosate, estimated to increase cancer risk by 41%, in playgrounds, schools and near homes. Christine Murray reports

Weedkiller being sprayed on a social housing garden. Photo: Alamy

An investigation by *The Developer* has revealed that 98% of councils use weedkillers containing glyphosate in 2018-19, with 97% applying it within 10 metres of private homes, schools, housing estates or playgrounds.

Glyphosate, the active ingredient in Monsanto's Roundup, is frequently used in towns and cities to stop the growth of plants on hard surfaces such as parking lots, footpaths, highways, fence lines, pavements, paths and brick walls in public urban spaces. It is considered the most-used herbicide in the world.

Researchers from the University of Washington recently estimated that glyphosate exposure increased the cancer risk of non-Hodgkin's lymphoma by 41%. In 2015, the World Health Organisation's International Agency for Research on Cancer classified glyphosate as "probably carcinogenic to humans".

In response to a Freedom of Information Act (FOIA) request, 316 out of 322 councils say they used a glyphosate-based weedkiller in 2018-19, with half having used a Roundup-branded product.

Where councils had responsibility for maintenance, 94% of FOIA responses from local authorities say they have used glyphosate on housing estates (253 out of 270); 69% used glyphosate on playgrounds (198 out of 288); and out of 179 councils, 61% (109) say they have used glyphosate on school grounds.

However, six councils say they do not use glyphosate: Hammersmith & Fulham, Lewes, North East Derbyshire ALMO (Rykneld Homes), Ryedale, Sevenoaks and Southampton. Lewes Council states that it will also be stopping the use of glyphosate in Eastbourne in future as the two councils have combined service provision.

Other councils say use of the herbicide is

"Glyphosate has been linked with a number of health issues, not only cancer. It is being sprayed, needlessly, in areas where children, potentially the most vulnerable to its harmful effects, live and play. There is a large enough body of evidence for the precautionary principle to be employed"

A Thames Water scientist testing for traces of pesticides in the River Cherwell

under review, with nine councils specifically stating that they are seeking to reduce their use of glyphosate and others are trialling alternative approaches.

The Pesticide Action Network says Brighton, Bristol, Derry and Trafford are adopting policies to significantly reduce and ultimately eliminate pesticide use, while Hackney and Croydon have also committed to reducing glyphosate use.

On 4 July, following *The Developer*'s revelation online in May about the widespread use of pesticides, the London Assembly adopted a motion calling on all London boroughs to stop using glyphosate on council property. It also called on mayor Sadiq Kahn to initiate a plan to eliminate glyphosate use on the Greater London Authority estate.

In March 2019, a federal jury in the US found that use of the glyphosate-based weedkiller Roundup had been "a substantial factor" in causing the cancer of a California former school groundskeeper in the second high-profile ruling to link Roundup with non-Hodgkin lymphoma.

In the wake of the US cases, the *Financial Times* reported that Bayer, which acquired Roundup manufacturer Monsanto last year for £63bn, faces "an avalanche of legal cases" estimated at around 14,000.

Bayer says its products pose no health risks. "Regulators worldwide continue to conclude, based on independent assessments, that glyphosate-based products can be used safely as directed and that glyphosate is not carcinogenic," Bayer told *The Developer*.

Councillor Wesley Harcourt, cabinet member for the environment at Hammersmith & Fulham Council, says: "Hammersmith & Fulham Council stopped the use of glyphosate on streets, estates and parks and open spaces two years ago based on health reasons as per the many reports from Europe and possible lawsuits in the US."

"We are now using steam and another hot foam method to remove weeds, along with some manual weeding where necessary. We have no intention of returning to glyphosate," Harcourt adds.

Hackney says it has "significantly" reduced its spraying on highways, although its FOIA response indicates a 66% increase in use on parks and green spaces. Fareham Borough Council has invested in foamstream treatment and weed-ripping machinery, while East Sussex Highways says it is currently looking into alternative methods.

Other councils appear entirely reliant on glyphosate, however, with 118 councils saying they use no alternative herbicides, mechanical or manual methods of weedkilling.

And while 90 councils have decreased their use of glyphosate in 2018-19 and 94 councils say their usage is unchanged, 68 councils say they have increased their use of the herbicide, with some citing the weather or Japanese knotweed as requiring more applications.

Asked to respond to the findings that some councils are moving away from glyphosate use, a spokesperson from Bayer says, "There is no evidence that local councils who choose to move away from glyphosate for amenity weed management are enhancing safety."

Glyphosate is approved for use in the UK until 2022.

Nick Mole, policy officer for the Pesticide Action Network UK, the charity behind the Pesticide-Free Towns initiative, expressed his alarm that so many councils are using glyphosate, saying: "There is cause for concern.

"Glyphosate has been linked with a number of health issues, not only cancer. It is being sprayed, needlessly, in areas where children, potentially the most vulnerable to its harmful effects, live and play," Mole says.

"There is a large enough body of evidence for the precautionary principle to be employed – not least because there are effective alternatives available."

The biggest spender on glyphosate is Norfolk, which spent £297,432 on glyphosate and its application including labour, followed by Camden Council, which spent £140,653, with Milton Keynes having spent £115,653 and Hackney £106,801 on the herbicide and its application.

The top three biggest users of glyphosate among the 297 local authorities that responded to the FOIA request are Milton Keynes at 11,065 litres, followed by South Tyneside at 9,860L (with 9,400L of this applied by South Tyneside Homes). Rushmoor is third at 8849.6L.

Other major users of glyphosate include Manchester, which used in excess of 6,040 litres at a cost of £50,598, followed by Durham (5,040L); Essex (5,015L); Wirral (4,485L); Aberdeenshire (4,343L); Rotherham (3,880L); Norfolk (3,875L);

Pesticide being spread on Blackfriars Street in Edinburgh. Photo: Alamy

Beekeepers have protested against the use of potentially harmful pesticides. Photo: Alamy

Dudley (3,840L); Sandwell (3,727L); Redcar & Cleveland (3,445L); Middlesbrough (3,250L); Northumberland (3,190L); Southwark (3,118L); Dundee City (2,754L); North Lanarkshire (2,715L); and Newham (2,700L).

Glyphosate's widespread use in city centres and public spaces is worrying, says Mole, because the number of people exposed in urban settings is greater, and glyphosate is also more likely to enter the water system.

"The main issue of hard-surface use is run-off," says Mole. "This is particularly problematic if glyphosate is applied in sub-optimal conditions such as rain or wind. But it is also an issue in general.

"Pesticides are mobile, and the run-off ends up in drains and water sources," adds Mole. "Decontaminating drinking water as a result of pesticide run-off adds to the bills we pay for our water, and harms aquatic ecosystems."

According to Thames Water's water quality reports for Camden and Hackney, the maximum pesticide count in these two London boroughs is very near the European legal limit, with a reading of 0.093μg/L – just 0.007 under the European legal limit of 0.1μg/L.

Phil Smart, inspector for the Drinking Water Inspectorate, says: "Although close to the legal limit, it is nevertheless below and presents no risk to health. Margins of error are taken care of as part of the analytical quality control process at the laboratory."

Bayer's Monsanto is under increased scrutiny following the release of internal documents as part of the US case, known as the Monsanto Papers. The company has been accused of seeking to influence regulators.

In 2017, the EU appeals committee controversially voted to re-authorise glyphosate for five years despite a petition signed by 1.3 million EU citizens calling for a ban. France and Vietnam have since sought to eliminate the use of glyphosate by banning its sale or import for domestic use.

Last year, *The Guardian* revealed that

EU regulators relicensed glyphosate based on a copy-and-pasted report presented as an independent assessment on the safety of glyphosate.

An investigation has been launched in France into Monsanto collecting information on 200 journalists, lawmakers and other individuals in the hope of influencing their position on pesticides.

The Monsanto Papers include an internal email revealed last month in which a Monsanto employee states that two of its employees are "working behind the scenes with UK government".

A second email states the need for a new dermal absorption study "because of a pending request from two authorities (UK, Denmark) in a zonal evaluation process in EU. If we use the default value, we do not pass the risk assessment".

In addition to health, there is concern that glyphosate is affecting biodiversity, insect populations, aquatic life and pollinators – a hot topic following the comprehensive recent report on biodiversity, *IPBES Global Assessment Report on Biodiversity and Ecosystem Services*.

Another recent study suggested glyphosate damages the beneficial gut bacteria in honeybees which makes them prone to infection.

Bayer's response reads: "Claims that glyphosate has a negative impact on honeybees are simply not true. Glyphosate and Roundup-branded herbicide products have been extensively tested in the laboratory and in the field to evaluate potential toxicity to honeybees."

Matt Shardlow, at conservation group Buglife, told *The Guardian* that "the biggest impact of glyphosate on bees is the destruction of the wildflowers on which they depend".

Among the councils that have responded

"Designing out pesticide is the best approach, avoiding cracks and corners where seeds can accumulate, using membranes and making areas more suitable for sweeping. We also need to move away from formal-type gardens and use more natural planting regimes, changing the mindset of what constitutes a weed"

to the FOIA to date, 63 say they used insecticides and 80 have used fungicides in addition to glyphosate-based weedkillers, adding to the chemical cocktail being applied by local authorities. Frequently used products included wasp and ant insecticides and fungicides for bowling greens and pitches.

Mole says there is no barrier to becoming a pesticide-free town: "Examples from around the world show it is possible to maintain towns and cities without the use of glyphosate, or other pesticides," he says.

"France has a complete ban on the use of non-agricultural pesticides, all of Belgium's towns and cities are managed without pesticides and there are hundreds more examples from around the world where this is happening in order to better protect the health of citizens and the environment."

Designing out pesticide is the best approach, Mole says, by avoiding cracks and corners where seeds and weeds can accumulate, using membranes beneath paving, and making areas more suitable for brushing and sweeping.

We need to rethink the aesthetics of public space, says Mole, "moving away from formal-type gardens and using more natural planting regimes, the creation of wildflower areas and changing the mindset about what constitutes a weed and the need to get rid of it".

Chris Brown, executive chair and founder of developer Igloo, agrees: "Urban rewilding, allowing natural ecosystems to re-establish, enhances the health and well-being benefits of public space."

Brown adds: "Who wouldn't be happier to hear the mellifluous song of a charm of goldfinches [who love thistles], or see the swooping flight of a summer's first swallow [who feed off flying insects], or taste delicious local urban honey [bee forage is the main constraint on urban bee populations]?"

As for local authorities, Mole says there are numerous good reasons to phase out the use of glyphosate: "Citizens want it, alternatives are available, and in the long term it could save them money."

Mole also says liability is a growing issue: "The current legal cases in the US are only the top of the iceberg.

"Thus far, a school groundskeeper and two members of the public have won cases against Monsanto for causing cancer as a result of exposure to glyphosate use," says Mole. "Could a council afford to take the chance of litigation and possible compensation?"

The online version of this article has been nominated for Scoop of the Year at the IBP Awards. The Developer has also been nominated for Editorial Brand of the Year

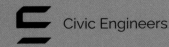

Tottenham is currently a hive of redevelopment. But a balance must be struck between regenerating the area and communities who have called this place home for many years

Helen Parton finds out whether developers have got the balance right, with photography from John Sturrock

Apex House, a new residential development by Grainger plc, in Seven Sisters, Tottenham

Football fans walking down Whitehall Street, going to a match at the new Tottenham Hotspur Stadium

Tottenham's cool credentials have been espoused by media outlets as varied as *The Daily Telegraph*, *Vice* magazine and *Condé Nast Traveller*.

Creative businesses have been attracted by cheaper rents than Dalston, nightclub goers by the lack of neighbours and developers by the former two groups signposting that this part of north London is, well, the new east London. Hazel Brown, editor of local magazine *Discovering Tottenham*, explains: "In the past few years, change has really ramped up. Tottenham has lots of creativity and so many new businesses, as well as many brilliant established small businesses – it's a real centre of opportunity. But the people here don't need another Shoreditch."

She points out that Northumberland Park, a ward within Tottenham, has high levels of poverty, borne out by Haringey Council's 'State of the Borough' survey. More than a third of people in Haringey live in poverty. Brown continues: "There is a strong, diverse community and I wanted to show that – it's important to make sure no one's left behind or priced out."

Rewind eight years and the area was attracting headlines for very different reasons than buzzy bars, craft breweries and the brand new Tottenham Hotspur Stadium. That was when the area felt the full force of the 2011 riots. Following the shooting of local resident Mark Duggan by Metropolitan Police officers, there were disturbances on Tottenham High Road, with that unforgettable image of Polish woman Monika Konczyk leaping from a burning building, one of several that caught ablaze that hot August night. Further back in older Tottenham residents' minds was the Broadwater Farm Estate riot in 1985 that occurred following the fatal heart attack of Cynthia Jarrett during a police search of her home. During the riot, one police officer, Keith Blakelock, was killed.

In 2012, a report was published entitled *It Took Another Riot* by the Independent Panel on Tottenham, which was chaired by property developer Sir Stuart Lipton. The report, which was commissioned by then-mayor of London Boris Johnson, made a number of recommendations for the area, among them improved housing and transport links and stronger relationships between the community and the police. Lipton urged the government, the Greater London Authority (GLA) and Haringey Council to invest, saying at the time: "Tottenham is a place which has been forgotten over the past 50 years. There hasn't been the driver to make this place into a community again." That same year, Johnson announced a £41m funding and investment package for Tottenham, which included £28m in GLA grants.

Housing also formed a significant part of the Haringey Development Vehicle (HDV), a 50:50 joint venture between the council and developer Lendlease, which in 2015 promised 6,400 homes over the next two decades as part of the redevelopment of several estates, among them Broadwater Farm and Northumberland Park. The £2bn scheme caused divisions within the council's ruling Labour party and following local elections in May 2018, the new administration, elected on a manifesto to cancel the HDV, did just that. It stated it "did not agree with the large-scale transfer of public assets out of public ownership, believing the council should retain its commercial portfolio".

Council leader Joseph Ejiofor said Haringey intended to build council homes, for council rent, on council land, delivering 1,000 in the borough by 2022. Lendlease, for its part, still has a presence in Tottenham at the High Road West development, providing more than 2,500 homes, including 191 replacement homes for council residents living on the Love Lane Estate near White Hart Lane Station, plus 200,000 sq ft of commercial, retail and leisure space.

Charles Adje, cabinet member for strategic regeneration at Haringey Council, explains the local authority's commitments. He talks of 72 new homes to be built by developers on the Red House site on West Green Road, 46 of which (64%) will be acquired by the council for social rent, and 131 council homes at council rents, part of the Argent Related development at Tottenham Hale with Housing Zone funding of over £100m, supporting the delivery of a number of new homes across north and south Tottenham. He also mentions a 10-year strategy for the High Road, "transforming the shops there to make them fit for purpose so that when you come out of Seven Sisters Station you want to engage with local businesses there".

This transport interchange, a tangle of Underground and Overground services to Liverpool Street one way and Cheshunt and Enfield the other, is an attack of the senses: the traffic of the busy A12, the bustle of West Green Road and not least Wards Corner, the site of a battle between developer Grainger plc and the Central and South American community, who have been trading there since the turn of the century. Through a doorway in between the Pueblito Paisa Cafe and a household goods shop and down a corridor, you enter what the Save Latin Village campaign organiser Mirca Morera describes as "the Victoria line to Latin America".

Inside, it is loud with conversations, mostly in Spanish, children running between the units, a mix of boutiques, nail bars, food outlets and money exchange services. "It's a real centre for Hispanic culture. People who wouldn't necessarily watch Tottenham Hotspur or go to the West End theatre or London's museums, they come here," Morera continues, explaining that many of those who have settled in the area are political refugees from Colombia, with nations such as Iran, Nigeria and Uganda represented here, too.

The redevelopment of Wards Corner dates back to 2004, with Haringey Council seeking a developer for a number of years. In 2012, it granted planning and conservation consent to Grainger for a mixed-use scheme including space for a new market, 196 flats and a shopping centre, plus public realm and landscaping. Grainger also gained planning for the redevelopment of nearby Apex House. The developer's plan is to temporarily relocate Latin Market traders into Apex House, decanting them back when Wards Corner is finished.

Johnny Kiddle, senior development manager at Grainger, says: "We are working closely with traders to provide reassurance. This includes a comprehensive package of financial support, including an initial three-month, rent-free period for traders at the temporary market, and a guarantee on rents for up to five years at the new market."

Morera counters that for many traders, "there's been a huge amount of investment for them, sometimes in the region of £20,000, and suddenly that asset's going to be replaced". She also says that because some of the units are on two floors – often with balconies, terraces and tiles that take their cues from the traditional Colombian style – the units offered in the new development are not necessarily like-for-like size-wise. Morera even went to Geneva to the United Nations, where human rights experts said it was "a threat to cultural life" if the redevelopment went ahead. The Wards Corner site was the subject of a compulsory purchase order (CPO), submitted by the council to the secretary of state for housing in 2016, which was confirmed in February 2019. The Latin Market community made an 11th-hour

> "The Latin Village is a real centre for Hispanic culture: people who wouldn't necessarily watch Tottenham Hotspur or go to the West End theatre or London's museums, they come here"

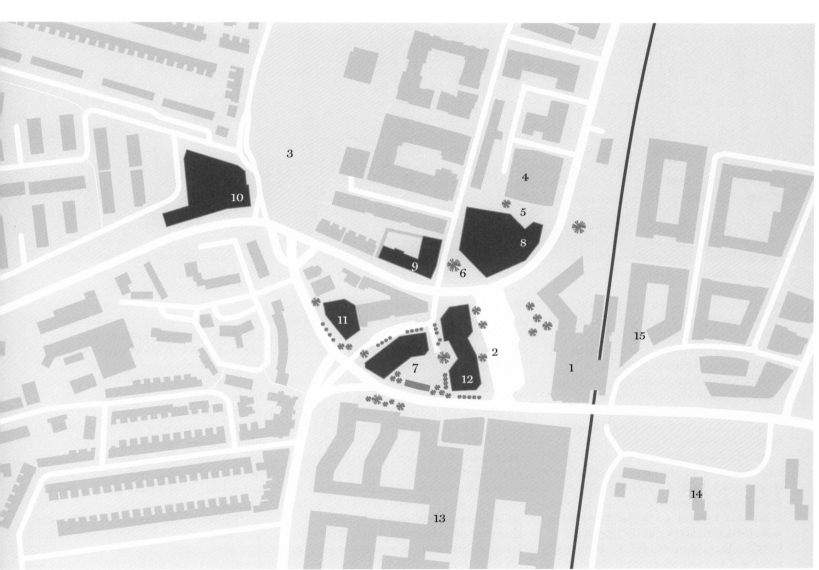

Argent Related's masterplan around Tottenham Hale Station: 1 Tottenham Hale Station 2 Bus station 3 Down Lane Park 4 National College for Digital Skills (Ada) 5 College Square 6 Watermead Place 7 Ferry Square 8 1 Ashley Road 9 2 Ashley Road 10 Welbourne 11 North Island 12 Ferry Island 13 Tottenham Hale Retail Park 14 Ferry Lane Estate 15 Unite student accommodation

Argent Related is regenerating Ashley Road near Tottenham Hale Station with 1,030 new homes, retail spaces and a paved public space

challenge to the CPO, but the High Court ruled against them, ordering traders to cover the £10k in legal costs.

Further up the road, Tottenham Green Market offers another food and drink destination, this one popping up every Sunday with local traders bringing an international flavour, from Downhills Park Jamaican patties to Romanian cake-makers Prestige Patisserie.

Marika Gauci, who has lived in the area for 20 years, set up the market in 2016. "I successfully tendered for it through Haringey's regeneration department. It was a nice space but it had no life and I thought it would be lovely to see it used," she says.

Gauci also started the Haringey Food and Drink Festival, which takes place every September, and last year attracted 8,000 locals. But keeping momentum for a weekly market is not easy, as Gauci explains: "I'm a fan of new business, but not a fan of oversaturation. Councils have to be careful not to harm the businesses it's helped already and the businesses that have been here for many years. We have suffered from too many markets opening in London, especially in the six-mile radius of Tottenham."

Hang a right down past Tottenham Green and onto Broad Lane and you reach Tottenham Hale, another hub of regeneration. Here, developer Argent

Related's plans are already well underway around Tottenham Hale Station. Its 1 Ashley Road building, designed by Alison Brooks Architects, is presently launching – its hot pink marketing suite hard to miss. A mix of studios plus one and two-bedroom apartments, prices start from £365,000. In total, the £500m masterplan includes 1,030 homes, of which 309 are for market sale, 482 build to rent, 108 shared ownership and the rest council homes that Haringey Council's Adje mentioned. The scheme also includes 15 new retail spaces, a health centre which will serve 30,000 people and two football pitches-worth of tree-lined, paved public space. As far as creating a sense of place for existing Tottenham residents goes, Tom Goodall, chief executive for the Tottenham Hale project, says: "The communities of people who already live in Tottenham are the first audience we need to impress and we want them to feel connected to the new spaces. We can't build in isolation and expect them to feel engaged in what we are collectively trying to achieve."

Lorna Reith has lived on the Ferry Lane Estate, which is adjacent to the Ferry Island part of Argent Related's project, since it was built in 1978. She says: "The buildings that are being knocked down [to make way for the new development] aren't things that people feel particularly wedded to."

The masterplan is replacing retail and light industrial spaces. She is, however, concerned about the preponderance of new, tall buildings in the area – Argent Related's plan represented six blocks at up to 38 storeys. "Around Ferry Lane, it used to be quite flat, but now I feel we've lost something." That said, she concedes: "I've been in local government, I've worked for both Haringey and Hackney councils, and I know we need much more council housing and houses that people can afford. You can either build up or build out and then you lose the green belt."

The lack of built-up residential areas up until now in Tottenham has been a boon

"The communities of people who already live in Tottenham are the first audience we need to impress and we want them to feel connected to the new spaces. We can't build in isolation and expect them to feel engaged in what we are trying to achieve"

Tottenham has had a number of popular late-night venues, such as The Cause on Ashley Road, due to the lack of built-up residential areas

for those seeking a late-night clubbing destination, just as well-known venues in central parts of the capital are closing and the 24-hour Victoria line began running to N17.

Stuart Glen has been running The Cause venue since spring 2018. "I've been putting on events for years. I got pushed out of Hackney as there were no spaces," he explains.

The former car mechanic depot on Ashley Road provides the perfect industrial backdrop to celebrate dance music culture. The venue has attracted a range of events from veteran American techno DJs to cult queer night Adonis. As well as night-time hedonism, The Cause does have the day-to-day community in mind too, supporting mental health charities Mind and CALM, and Help Musicians UK, and the building is home to local radio station Threads.

When time is up on this meanwhile space – the last hurrah is a New Year's Eve spectacular – would Glen like to stay in the area? "I would but there aren't any buildings left!" he says. A throwaway comment, perhaps, but one that resonates with the end-of-an-era feeling from the rumble of trucks and the army of high-vis-clad contractors in and around Tottenham Hale Station.

One creative entrepreneur hoping to get in on the act of Tottenham's cache is Mary Otumahana, who writes and performs as a

rapper under the name WondRWomN. She set up the The Record Shop, which provides free recording sessions for 16 to 25-year-olds, in 2015. Otumahana has a background in youth work and that, coupled with her own experience of not being able to afford recording space herself, encouraged her to set up the enterprise. As well as helping scores of local young people develop their music careers, Otumahana has also collaborated with the likes of O_2 and Red Bull.

"There's a very entrepreneurial culture within the community," she says. "Lots of brands are interested in working with people in the area. These companies have a corporate social responsibility role in supporting local creativity." Otumahana also continues to do WondRWomN gigs, many locally. "It's a balance between performing and running a business," she explains.

Hers was one of the faces that appeared during the launch of Tottenham Hotspur's new kit in August, a couple of months after the launch of the new stadium itself.

Beyond the eye-catching statistics – the biggest club stadium in London, Europe's longest bar – there are touches which ring true to Tottenham chair Daniel Levy's claim to provide "an unrivalled fan experience and significant benefits to our local community". The media room, which looks more like a trendy co-working space, is used as a cafe

on non-game days and Grade II listed Warmington House has been transformed into a museum and heritage centre.

The second planned phase of the project also includes a community health centre and 222 new affordable homes. The stadium is not just intended for the English iteration of football but the pitch can be retracted so the American version can be played on artificial turf beneath the grass.

Concerts and other events can be hosted here too, filling the gap between the capacities of Wembley and the O_2, explains Christopher Lee, managing director at Populous, the architect behind the scheme.

On a sweltering June evening this year, Tottenham's football team were in Madrid playing the Champions League Final and the stadium showed the match. Walking up the High Road from Seven Sisters, people of all ages and ethnicities filled the street, all with a palpable sense of optimism, even if the result didn't go their way.

Cafe in the Latin Village, Wards Corner – this area is the centre of a dispute between locals and Grainger, which has plans to demolish it

Distinctive buildings near Seven Sisters Station, controversially due for demolition to make way for a high-rise residential building

A hair studio on the High Road – there is a 10-year strategy to "transform the shops" next to Seven Sisters Station, according to a local councillor

Lorna Reith, on the balcony of her flat on the Ferry Lane Estate beside the River Lea. The estate is adjacent to Argent's big Ferry Island project

Youngsters playing ball games on Cruyff Court, beside the Ferry Lane Estate in Tottenham Hale

Sunday lunchtime at Tottenham Green Market – traders are wary of new retail harming existing businesses that have been there many years

Markfield Road, a street off Broad Lane – Broad Lane leads up to Tottenham Hale Station in one direction and Seven Sisters in the other

Residents chat on the Ferry Lane Estate – Argent Related's Ferry Island scheme has plans for six high rises up to 38 storeys next to the estate

Aerial view of Tottenham Hale, with Tottenham Hotspur Stadium in the distance

Involving communities in the design of homes

Design Council's **Sarah Weir** explains the importance of a 'whole-place' approach and the five key principles unpinning development that a group of young architects developed at this year's inaugural Festival of Place

Design Council has long been advocating for a 'whole-place' approach to how we plan our housing, communities, towns and cities. We believe that taking a broader and much more inclusive approach is the only way to ensure we're integrating the diverse needs of today's population into new plans and developments, right from the outset. This will enable us to build safe, high-quality and sustainable homes and environments that encourage healthier and happier lifestyles and truly cater for the people who will live in them long after the developers have left.

That's why being part of the inaugural Festival of Place in July was a refreshing experience. As the name suggests, the aim was to create a forum to discuss 'place' – not housing, infrastructure, transport, sustainability or any other element in isolation, but all these factors and many others in combination – to inform how we plan and build the homes and communities of the future.

There were sessions on climate change, working with communities, smart cities, crime, social inequality, designing child-friendly environments and many other elements that make up the kind of whole-place approach that Design Council supports.

My talk at the festival was on the importance of inclusive design, which bridges all the different factors and considerations that go into a whole-place approach. An inclusive environment is created from conversations early in the process with a wide range of people who will live and use the place, ensuring it is aligned to everyone's needs. As a result, it can be used safely, easily and with dignity by all. It is convenient, welcoming and provides independent access without additional undue effort, separation or special treatment for any group of people.

Ultimately, inclusive design ensures that the diverse needs of the population are accommodated and gives everyone the same choices, freedoms and experiences.

Our session with young architecture students unpacked further how we can be better at designing with a whole-place approach and with inclusivity in mind. Encouragingly, conversations about housing in isolation didn't come up at all.

Five key pillars of inclusive design emerged from our brainstorming. The first, a people-first approach, moves the planning and developing process away from consultations to conversations. Communities are involved from the outset, by discussing with them what they need from new developments and giving them a sense of ownership over where they live.

The second is that diversity should be at the core of inclusive design. A place should reflect the values of all the people who live in it. Having conversations with all parts of the community will allow the needs of all demographics to be catered for.

Inclusively designed places should also promote people's health and well-being, and support the environment. This means access to green and blue spaces, prioritising cycling and pedestrianisation, limiting the effects of air pollution, limiting the use of cars where appropriate, and providing good access to public transport.

Ambitions for more inclusively designed places need the right education and legislation in place to bring them to fruition. This means upskilling and training in industry and government, as well as educating the public about how they can play a role in the future of their communities.

Lastly, we need to ensure communities feel more empowered about where they live and know they have a voice in how it's being shaped. This, coupled with high-quality and sustainable design, will ensure that we build spaces that endure and that people want to remain in for their lifetime.

There are already some excellent examples of these approaches that deserve to be

Sarah Weir, speaking at the Festival Place. Photo: John Sturrock

Access to green spaces is important. Photo: Simon Dewhurst Photograp

"An inclusive environment is created from conversations early in the process with a wide range of people who will live and use the place, ensuring it is aligned to everyone's needs. As a result, it can be used safely, easily and with dignity by all"

Bradford's City Park. Photo: Tim Green

acknowledged. Bromley by Bow Health Centre in London was founded in 1984 as the UK's first healthy living centre, combining psychologists, nurses and counsellors with artists, stonemasons, gardeners and other community support and activities – diverse services for a diverse population.

Bradford's City Park reclaimed a key area of the city centre as a people-first meeting place for locals, who have embraced it. It has now become an award-winning symbol of the city's regeneration ambitions, boosting local business and investment.

Meanwhile, LILAC is a co-housing community of 20 eco-build households in west Leeds, managed by residents through a mutual homeownership society. This new financial model ensures permanent affordability. The project, which is suitable for rolling out elsewhere, combines all the pillars of inclusive design highlighted here.

Back at the Festival of Place, the Pineapple Awards, which Design Council proudly sponsored, focused on celebrating new and thriving urban developments in the UK where people really want to live, work, play, shop or learn. It was encouraging to see such a variety of entries that really had put people and place at the heart of their design.

The Borough of Camden's West End project, creating safer, greener and more attractive streets for residents and visitors, and Leeds' bold South Bank regeneration project spring to mind.

The only downside was the small proportion of entries from outside London and the South East. We need to do more to encourage people from all regions to be involved in and promoting schemes and initiatives like this.

The Festival of Place was a superb platform for us all to share our stories about developing inclusive environments. We are encouraged by the discussions we have had. We now return, with renewed vigour, to our challenge of ensuring all those working in architecture and the built environment adopt a whole-place, inclusive approach, highlighting the transformative impact it can have – now and well into the future.

Five pillars of inclusive design

1. A people-first approach
2. Diversity at the core
3. Health, well-being and the environment
4. Education and legislation
5. Empowerment and longevity

Marmalade Lane in Cambridge is the site of a successful cohousing project

But how did the council and residents work together to overcome the challenges that so often mean these schemes fail? Laura Mark visits the development to see how a resilient, intergenerational community has been established, more than a decade after plans were first drawn up. Photography by David Christian

The Marmalade Lane cohousing project features a mixture of families with young children, older residents and young professionals

Cambridge Council couldn't find a buyer for the plot but gained funding and drew up a brief for the site with the K1 housing group

Just 15 minutes' cycle from Cambridge city centre lies Marmalade Lane, an urban idyll of 42 brick-clad homes with car-free streets, where children play football and draw chalk murals. It stands in stark contrast to the surrounding suburban cul-de-sacs of the Orchard Park Estate, designed 10 years ago to be aspirational but now dubbed 'Beirut' by residents.

Marmalade Lane is a plot left over from that previous housing development and wouldn't have happened if it hadn't been for the recession. In 2008, the developers for the site walked away leaving a plot (known as K1) which Cambridge Council struggled to find anyone else to develop. It decided to allocate the plot to cohousing and was successful in gaining funding from the Homes and Communities Agency (now Homes England) to draw up a brief with the K1 cohousing group.

But for this to work, they needed the equity from a development partner so the residents wouldn't spend all their money on buying the land – the biggest barrier for cohousing groups is always land cost and availability.

So in 2014, armed with a 60-page brief drawn up by the K1 cohousing group, the council held a two-stage developer-led competition. The winning developer would have to work with the cohousing community and local planning authority to complete the final design, and fund and deliver the development.

From a shortlist of three, the final stage was won by a team made up of relatively new developer Town, Swedish offsite timber manufacturer Trivselhus, and architecture practice Mole.

Meredith Bowles, founder of Mole, comments that this is a fairly unusual model for a cohousing scheme: "This is not the way most cohousing schemes go. This was more like a normal housing project due to the procurement."

At the time of the developer competition, there were around 20 households who were members of the cohousing group, of which around 15 remain and have moved into the built scheme.

"Sticking to the brief rigidly became secondary as we were evolving the plans," comments Jonny Anstead, founding director of Town. "But this could only happen after trust with the cohousing group had been developed. If it had been a more cynical developer, the brief they had already developed would have been more important."

According to Mole, the scheme differs in some ways from that initially briefed. Cars were originally placed around the outside of the site and the scheme was a lot more inward looking, but this was reversed with the creation of the internal car-free street and by moving the common house to the centre of the plan, giving it a relationship with the garden.

They also worked to rationalise the types of homes on offer. The architects developed three different house types, which could then be configured with up to 27 different internal layouts. These are all the same depth so can be positioned anywhere along a terrace while the width can vary. This allowed residents choice and the ability to configure their own homes to their needs while keeping the costs down and allowing for offsite timber construction.

These design changes were worked out with residents over a four-month period through workshops. The cohousing group had working groups that focused on the houses, landscaping, energy use and common spaces, and they all met with the architects and developer on a regular basis and fed back to the rest of the community.

"We only met with the full group of residents a couple of times," says Bowles. "It was brilliantly organised and they made decisions efficiently based on consensus. As there were different members in each group it felt like we met with a lot of them regularly."

But there were some frustrations with this process.

"Once we had won the competition, the developer had committed to the cost of the scheme. It meant that the amount that could be changed was pretty limited. This was slightly frustrating," comments Bowles. "It would have been nice to have spent more time with the residents early on."

"I can see why some developers don't want to know their end users. When you do you worry about them and it becomes more personal," says Anstead. "This is a whole

"I can see why some developers don't want to know their end users. When you do you worry about them and it becomes more personal. This is a whole new way of doing it. Developers should have contact with those living in their homes and that would change the context of housing today"

new way of doing it. Developers should have contact with those living in their homes and that would change the context of housing today."

At Marmalade Lane, all residents have a share of the common house – the central space that includes a large catering kitchen, dining room, yoga studio, gym, library, laundry and guest bedrooms. Originally this space was briefed to be twice the size but during the design process they took stock of what was really needed and how it would be managed. Financial costs are shared and kept down by the expectation that residents will take part in a cleaning rota and a quarterly work day.

"All of our shared areas are great and we are finding ways to use them, but the more shared areas you have the more maintenance and cleaning you need to do," comments resident Lora Brill, when asked what advice she would give to other groups planning their communal spaces.

"There is so much communal space that we use parts of it and not other parts," she adds. "We use the lane behind our houses heavily. My son loves to play football out there. I go to yoga and pilates in the common house."

It is this lane which seems to be one of the most popular spaces. Although the first time I visit it is a rainy, grey day there is still a child playing and there are trikes, bicycles and other toys scattered around. I'm told if you are there after school it is filled with all the kids from the housing.

The success of this lane partly lies in the overlooking aspect: on one side, front doors open directly onto it, while on the other, the houses' back gardens adjoin the lane separated by just low walls and hedges. It will be interesting to see whether residents keep it this way or decide to let their hedges grow higher or add fences or more greenery. But the shared nature of an intentional community like this suggests that for it to thrive and remain as open and welcoming as it currently is, there has to be a blurred line between public and private.

Cohousing first became recognised in the 1970s when intentional communities, often with a social and environmental ethos, formed in Denmark. It slowly spread across Europe and now 7% of all housing in Denmark is cohousing and Germany also has a similar system called 'baugruppen' (meaning group build), where the council provides bridging finance and identifies sites.

"We went to Copenhagen and the Netherlands and looked at cohousing there, and the radical difference is the attitude to private space," says Bowles.

Once the reserve of hippy-types and seen

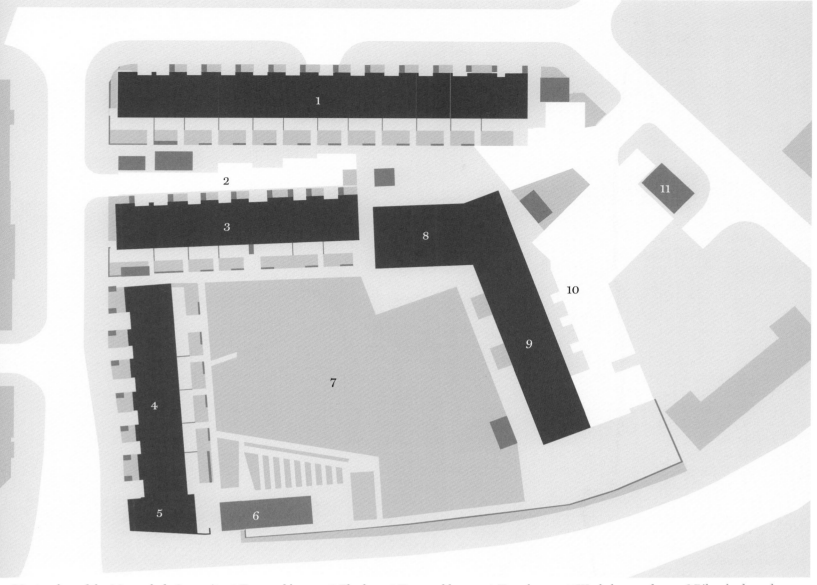

Masterplan of the Marmalade Lane site: 1 Terraced houses 2 The lane 3 Terraced houses 4 Townhouses 5 Workshop and gym 6 Bike sheds and garden storage 7 Shared garden 8 The common house 9 Apartment building 10 Car parking 11 Electricity substation

as a milder version of communes and housing co-operatives, cohousing is gaining traction. In particular, we are seeing it being targeted at older homeowners as a way to tackle the loneliness epidemic. In 2017, *Saga Magazine* even published an article encouraging its audience of mainly pensioners to consider the housing type.

Marmalade Lane resident Jan Chadwick and her husband decided to move to the estate after reading an article on cohousing in *The Guardian*: "We started to think about our situation, as 60-year-olds. With one daughter, and no desire to become dependent older parents, we saw cohousing as a potential solution to ensure we stayed interested, lively and engaged in our community, now and during our twilight years."

But at Marmalade Lane, which houses a mixture of families with young children, retired couples and young professionals, it is the families who really feel they benefit.

"The voices of women with children doesn't seem to get heard by the housing industry. But here it is safe," comments resident Frances Wright. "It has become an easier place for families and young mothers with children to live as there is support."

"It makes it much easier to parent, frankly. It means you aren't constantly trying to entertain your children yourself. There are other kids for them to play with. We hardly ever need to go to the park any more because we have so much space here," adds Brill.

There are around 20 residents under the age of 10 who live within the scheme. Having the extra space for children to play outside in the lane, the gardens or even the common house takes the pressure off families having children crammed inside each other's houses.

Of the residents I speak to, many have jobs with an environmental or social conscious focus, and it is easy to wonder whether the move towards these types of more shared developments is something being driven by the liberal elite.

"My interest in community housing comes from various sources, but predominantly my work for Argyle Street Housing Co-operative. Seeing it in action really made me want to live in an intentional community myself," says resident Hannah Shields.

"My main driver has always been the children. I really feel that cohousing will be hugely beneficial to them, with increased freedom and a sense of extended family. I also think growing up in a community where tolerance, respect and compromise are practised through consensus decision-making will be a fantastic education in how to be an active member of society.

"I love the idea of our four children having so many adults beyond ourselves with whom to engage and learn from."

Brill adds: "You go into jobs related to sustainability and social justice because you care about those things. Here you can have a cohesiveness between your work life and your home life."

Marmalade Lane isn't a one-off. It is among 20 schemes in existence in the UK,

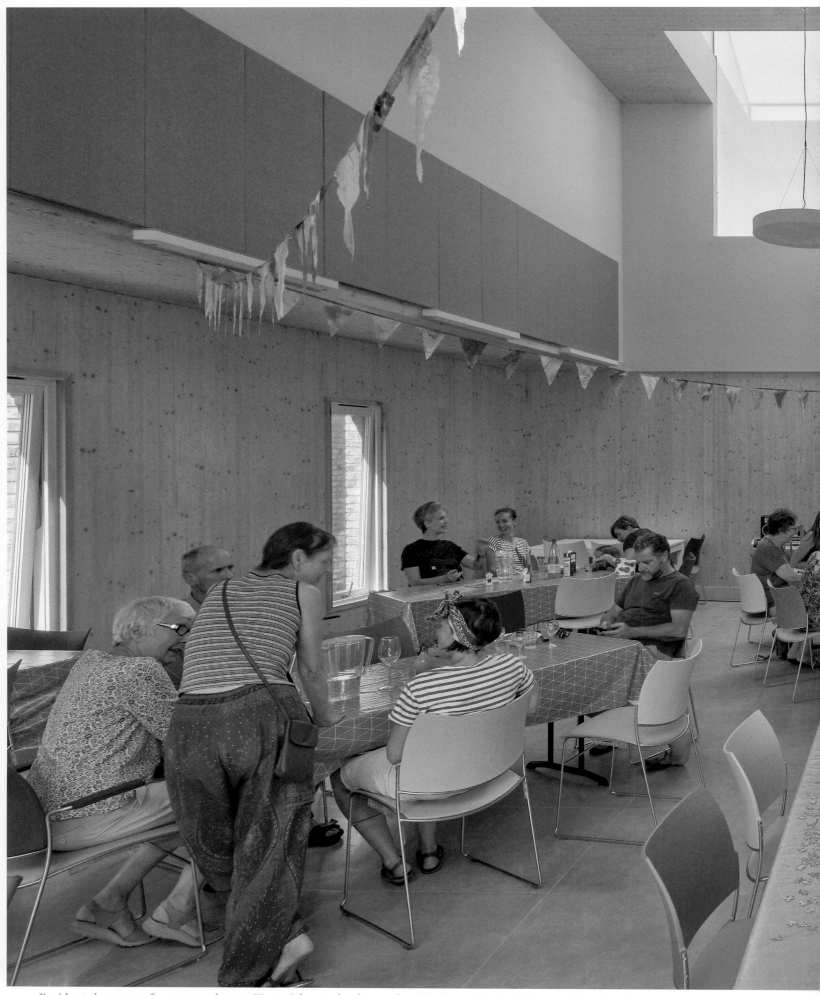

Residents have use of a common house. Financial costs for this are kept low by residents taking part in a cleaning rota

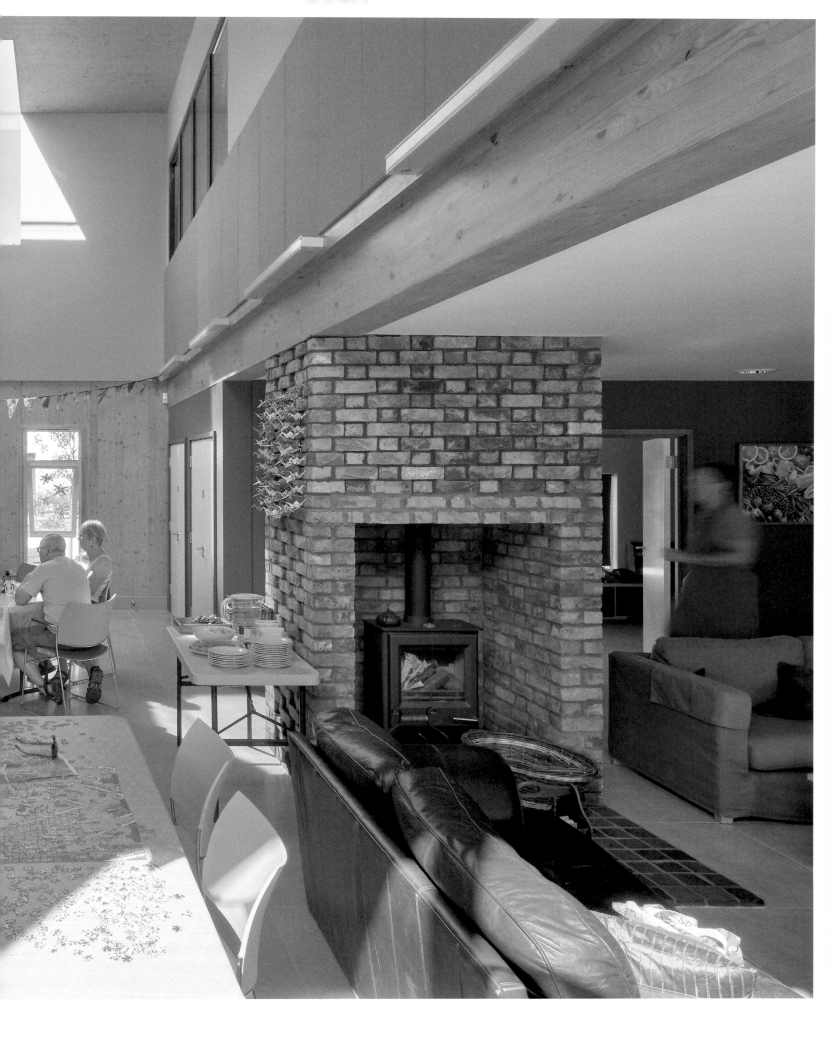

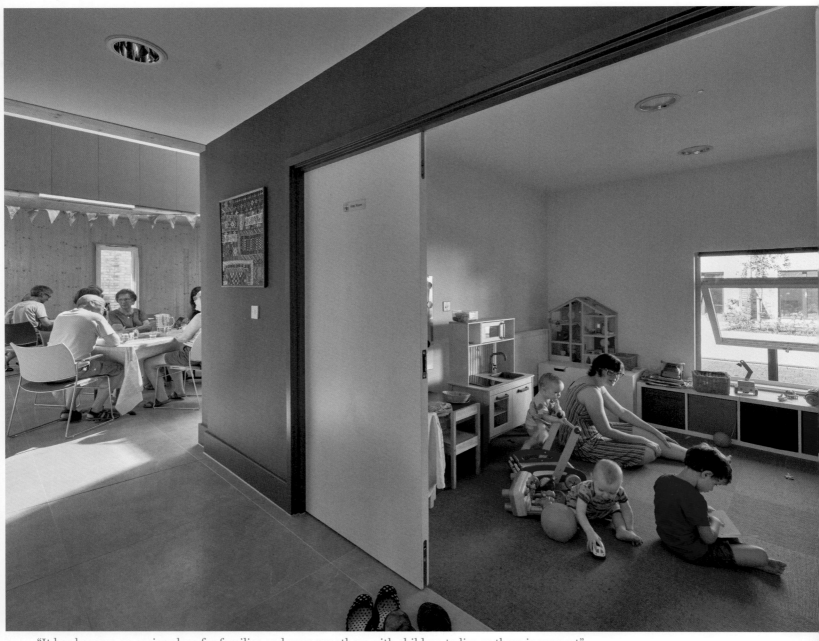

"It has become an easier place for families and young mothers with children to live as there is support"

including the well-known projects Lancaster Cohousing on the outskirts of Preston, Low Impact Living Affordable Community (LILAC) in Leeds, and the Older Women's Cohousing community in north London.

But it is one of the lucky schemes that did get off the ground. Cambridge K1 Cohousing originally formed in 2000 but struggled to find a plot and many projects are getting lost during this process of finding land. According to the UK Cohousing Network, there are currently 60 groups waiting to get started.

"Making land available for groups that are motivated would mean that more cohousing would happen. It is so hard to get land and to start the development process. Groups can spend a decade trying to create cohousing and that's really such a waste of valuable energy and time. It could happen so much faster if land was made available," adds Brill.

"The barriers to cohousing are usually wholly financial," says Bowles. "People can

overcome the organisational difficulties but the first hurdle is always land."

Bowles adds: "It needs local authority intervention. They could intervene through the planning system or by making land available."

For the residents of Marmalade Lane it has taken 20 years to get to this point. With prices ranging from £195,000 for a one-bedroom apartment to £535,000 for a five-bedroom house and with no requirement for building any affordable homes, this isn't housing which is open to all and it isn't going to solve the housing crisis. But it does provide an example of what can be done when a council releases land and a community gathers together and sticks with the process.

In Cambridge this type of community-led development was a last resort, a decision made by a fairly forward-thinking council when it knew it wasn't going to be able to develop the site in the usual way. Town, the

developer, is now working with 12 other cohousing groups where it will take forward what it has learned on this scheme. So, for other cities this has the potential to really challenge our traditional methods of bringing forward housing. But it will only work with planning and land-system changes.

Let's take a lesson from Germany's baugruppen and perhaps then streets where children play, common spaces with shared dinners, and truly intergenerational communities will become a positive outcome of the housing crisis.

Laura Mark is an award-winning architecture critic, curator and filmmaker. She is currently the keeper at Walmer Yard – a set of four houses in Notting Hill designed by Peter Salter – where she runs the Baylight Foundation, a charitable organisation with the aim of increasing the public's understanding of what architecture can do

To make a success of a project like this, there must be a blurred line between public and private space

There are 20 residents under 10 years old living within the scheme.

Having the extra overlooked, car-free communal space means more outdoor play for children

The lane is a popular place for children to play, with bikes, trikes and scooters scattered around the area

Fifteen households remain from the original 20-strong cohousing group set up in 2008

The scheme features a car-free street and original residents were offered three different house types which could be laid out in 27 ways

Glasgow's iconic Sauchiehall Street is in decline

Jessica Cargill Thompson finds out how planners, locals and investors are trying to revitalise the shopping district, with photography from Murdo MacLeod

Pedestrians walk past the boarded-up BHS shop-front. The store closed a couple of years ago but there is a 12-storey block planned for the site

The Avenues project for the district provides more greenery, segregated cycle lanes, more pedestrian space and decreases clutter

COLAB inside the Savoy Centre has tried to bring colour to the area and mixes start-ups with established traders

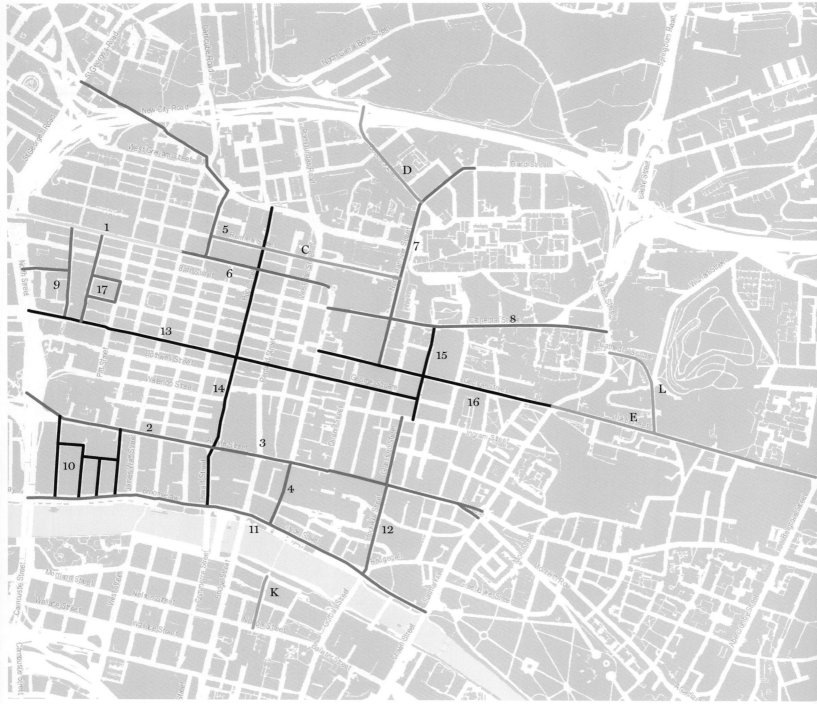

The Avenues project

Pilot scheme	**Block A**	**Block B**	**Block C**	**Block S**
1 Sauchiehall Street West	2 Argyle Street West	9 Elmbank Street - Elmbank Crescent	10 IFSD West	C Renfrew Street/ Killermont Street
	3 Argyle Street East - Trongate	11 Broomielaw - Clyde Street	13 St Vincent Street	D Dobbies Loan
	4 St Enoch Square - Dixon Street	12 Glassford Street/ Stockwell Street	14 Hope Street/Oswald Street	E Duke Street - Bellgrove Street
	5 The Underline (including Cambridge Street)	17 Holland Street/Pitt Street	15 John Street	K South Portland Street
	6 Sauchiehall Street Precinct		16 George Street	L John Knox Street (Duke Street - Castle Street)
	7 North Hanover Street - Kyle Street			
	8 Bath Street East - Cathedral Street			

Glasgow's Sauchiehall Street district must be cursed. First there was the widely publicised fire in 2014 that struck the Charles Rennie Mackintosh building at the Glasgow School of Art (GSA). Then followed a major conflagration in popular nightclub Victoria's in March 2018, which took out most of that block. Finally, and most painfully, a second fire at GSA devastated the building, throwing restoration into question.

Collateral has included the art deco O₂ ABC cinema that backed onto the art school, now scheduled for demolition but which sparked a passionate campaign to save it, and the temporary closure of several streets, all taking a toll on the local community. One long-standing local trader – one of the only independents left on the main drag – says he knows 30 independent businesses that have gone under; in 2018, the city's *Evening Times* reported 75 empty retail units.

Although the fires loom large in popular discourse about the city's misfortunes, the Sauchiehall Street neighbourhood is a familiar example of city-centre decline, exacerbated by national economic malaise and globally changing shopping habits – a strip where the glittering prizes of John Lewis and co swiftly peter out into Poundlands, phone shops and empty sites.

Look above this dispiriting scene and you see the street that once was – imposing sandstone facades in the fashionable architectural styles of their day, once housing the department stores that served the city's wealthy mercantile classes. Grand buildings that are simultaneously heritage assets and drains on maintenance budgets, crying out for forward thinking, creatively minded investors to take them on and reinvent them for the 21st century. Those that limp on, such as Watt Brothers, celebrating its centenary, have the air of the last days of a closing down sale, yet there is talk that even they might be selling up their city centre site.

But Glasgow is a tough, proud city and it doesn't give up that easily. There is a confidence that the area can be successful again – Glasgow's city centre as a whole is still the UK's number one retail centre outside London's West End. What might that success look like? And who or what will end up as collateral damage?

Jane Laiolo, group manager for city centre regeneration at Glasgow City Council, says: "People want to see Sauchiehall Street returned to what it used to be. It was big department stores and it was the premier shopping street. But those days are gone. Retail of those days is gone. The demands from retail investors has changed since the crash in 2008. Anyone who thinks we can return the city centre to that is not fully

The Watt Brothers department store – the grand building is a reminder of a bygone era

understanding of economic trends.

"We want to support the district. We want to return it to a street that people aren't disappointed by – that you would go to on a Saturday night or a Saturday afternoon."

To this end, the council has made the Sauchiehall Street area the first of eight districts to complete a regeneration framework as part of its 10-year city centre strategy, launched in 2013-14. Laiolo says there are more than 52 different regeneration strategies affecting the city centre: at Sauchiehall Street £7.2m has been spent on public realm improvements, part of a wider £115m Avenues project of walkable cyclable routes across the city; in addition, a city centre-wide upper-floors policy seeks to fill the underused spaces above the shop units, with a view to increasing city centre living from the current 20,000 residents to 35,000 by 2030.

Lead designer of the Avenues project is Urban Movement, and Christopher Martin, its director of urban strategy, says: "Something that we have taken forward in the design of Sauchiehall Street and the Avenues in general is to shape the city… as a catalyst for social inclusion, shared prosperity, healthy lifestyles and enjoyment.

"The way Glasgow's streets and public realm has been shaped has undoubtedly led to challenges… with 25% of land in the city centre being given over to vehicles and not people, compared with 18% in Manchester, 14% in Newcastle, and only 12% in Edinburgh."

The Sauchiehall Street district is a neighbourhood of mixed uses, a cluster of possible tensions, but also a rich base waiting to be activated. Walk one street north up

the hill from the main retail drag and you are amid the relatively quiet residential neighbourhood of Garnethill, with its four-storey tenements, Catholic high school and local park. One street south is genteel Bath Street, with private art galleries and bespoke wedding outfitters. A couple more streets along and you hit the prime office district of St Vincent Street. Up against all of this rubs a famous night-time economy that accommodates rowdy bars, student dives and famous clubs, as well as several theatres and cinemas.

New projects and forward-thinking developers are recognising the potential of this diversity, taking big buildings in hand and reimagining how they might be used, acting as possible catalysts for wider change in the area.

Inside the Savoy Centre (140 Sauchiehall Street) – Glasgow's oldest indoor market – the two floors of retail units had become something of a backwater, but a new initiative by the Savoy Centre's owner is attempting to bring colour, activity, and

CGI of Argyle Street, part of the Avenues project. Image: Ian Hingley

A painted mural featuring kittens at a gap site in the Sauchiehall Street area

The art deco O₂ ABC cinema on Sauchiehall Street is scheduled for demolition, despite a campaign to save it

Cycle lanes are an important element of the regeneration of the Sauchiehall Street area with the Avenues project

Sauchiehall Street is the first of eight districts in Glasgow that will complete a 10-year regeneration framework

Garnethill, north of Sauchiehall Street – the Avenues project will make it easier to connect this area with the rest of the city

Sauchiehall Street is the number one retail district in the UK outside of London's West End

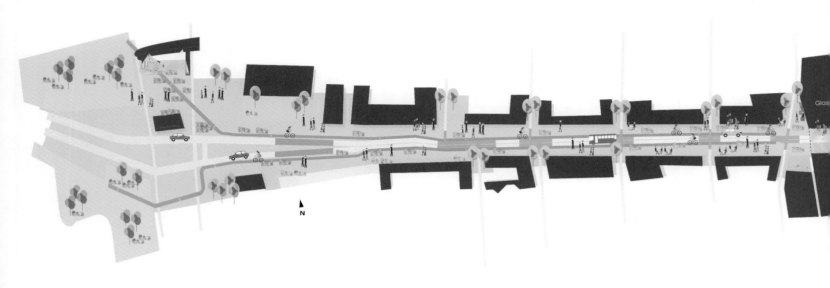

Masterplan of the Avenues project for Argyle Street, courtesy of Urban Movement

a new generation of patrons into the space. Called COLAB and launched last December, it sits hip start-ups (a Poke cafe, art installations and streetwear designers) cheek-by-jowl with established traditional traders (a Turkish barber, Scottish butcher, Chinese herbalist). In particular it is working closely with the arts community and has become home to the new Glasgow Gallery of Photography. After hours there might be live music events; at weekends market stalls, wellness workshops and vinyl fairs; and at the rear of the building an art platform of commissioned exhibitions animating a particularly gloomy stretch of Renfrew Street.

"We are looking to create a traditional central market unlike any other market in Scotland, incorporating a mix of retail, community, culture, art and cuisine," says Natalia Codona, project manager at COLAB. "It's a place to reintegrate families back into the city centre by creating a wide offering of free arts and crafts, activities, and entertainment.

"Given the recent tragedies on Sauchiehall Street, it's not only the Savoy Market needing attention but the street in general. COLAB

is the beginning of the rebirth of Sauchiehall Street."

While COLAB says its ethos is "collaboration over competition" and values its mix of old and new tenants, the white cubes of COLAB stick out from its neighbours, and not everyone feels like they are part of this brave new collaboration.

"The demands from retail investors has changed since the crash. Anyone who thinks we can return the city centre to that is not understanding of economic trends. We want to return it to a street that people aren't disappointed by – that you would go to on a Saturday night or a Saturday afternoon"

Some of the long-time traders, especially those who have been asked to move to the first floor, feel cut off thanks to a long-term broken escalator and have expressed fears of being gentrified out of the space; Glasgow's *Evening Times* has reported that many feel pushed out because they do not "fit into the COLAB aesthetic".

Paul Abrahams, who has been running second-hand bookseller The Book Tree since the 1960s, is happy to make room for the new – as long as everyone is included. "The days of the 5,000-10,000 sq ft shop are gone. The only thing you can do with these buildings is to subdivide them and revert back to the entrepreneurial ideology of 100 years ago. Give people coming out of the art school and the universities the opportunity to do their own thing."

A couple of blocks further west, backing onto the GSA's McLellan Galleries, Bywater Properties has bought a whole block to provide flexible office space for a creative SME crowd. McLellan Works, as it is being marketed, is a commercial departure for an area that is outside the traditional office district and renowned as down on its luck.

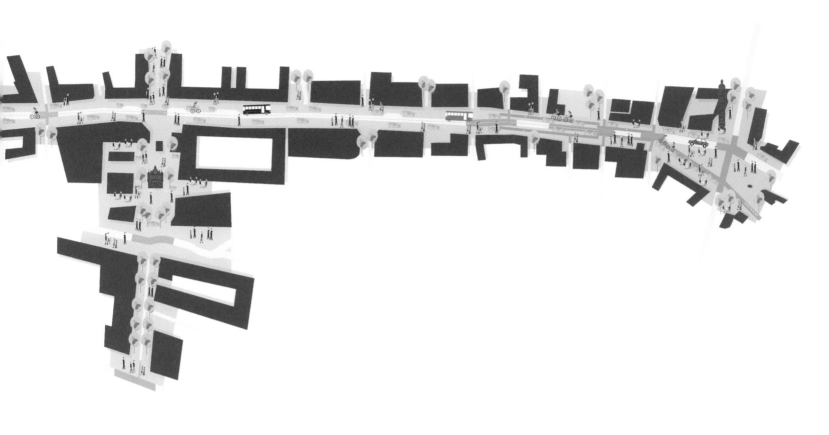

"We like down on its luck, because that's where interesting things emerge," says Theo Michell, principal at Bywater. "This is still a primary location with John Lewis at one end of the street and then at the far end [across the M8] bleeding off down to [foodie quarter] Finnieston and the West End, and the major powerhouse of the Glasgow School of Art right in the middle of it behind you. St Vincent Street may be the core office district but occupiers are beginning to realise that staff want to work in the places that are down on their luck, where things are sprouting up, not in relatively sanitised grade A areas."

The building (Breckenridge House, 274 Sauchiehall Street) was once home to department store Tréron et Cie, but only the neoclassical facade is original due to another fire, this time back in the 1990s. The interior will be 'defurbed' this summer, stripped out to leave exposed ceilings and services, leaving two floors of subdivided office space aimed at small to medium creative enterprises, sitting above street level retail and a basement gym and bike storage.

Bywater is discussing a symbiotic relationship with its rear neighbour whereby the office spaces lend creative energy from the world-renowned institution, while the art school gains a route through the building and a valuable front-door presence on Sauchiehall Street. In addition, some commercial units could be used for teaching, especially while the Mackintosh building is out of action, and there is a double-height lobby space used for exhibitions and a coffee shop – an extension of the outdoor street.

"It enlivens what's going on upstairs and speaks to the overall spirit of the project and the bits the public don't easily see, ie the upper floors."

New tenants are expected to be in place in spring 2020. Activation of the ground-floor retail spaces focuses on the prominent corner site where Bywater is looking at less traditional rental agreements to encourage a more entrepreneurial tenant – good for the chef, good for the area, and sending out a strong message of intent to potential office tenants. "There's increasingly a theme across retail of partnering with operators on a revenue share basis," says Michell, "so one of the ideas we've been kicking around is putting together what a restaurant might need, then offering it on a residency type basis to, say, a Finnieston restaurateur who wants to try out a new concept, or a frustrated sous chef looking to make a leap and do their own thing without the burden of a five-year lease. We want it to be local and entrepreneurial, which at the end of the day is the main commercial imperative from our point of view."

While McLellan Works, COLAB and others work on individual blocks, these islands need to be joined up with spaces people want to be in and pass through. To make the city centre more people-friendly and attract investment, the city council's Avenues project connects 17 streets across the city centre (including Argyle Street pictured above) and under the troublesome barrier of the M8 motorway, reducing space for private vehicles, planting green infrastructure, creating segregated cycle lanes, improving street lighting, introducing smart infrastructure (such as free wi-fi), and leading people through the city centre via this new landscape. The Sauchiehall Street improvements were completed in summer – replacing two of the four traffic lanes with

Paul Abrahams in his bookshop in COLAB in the Savoy Centre. His business has been on Sauchiehall Street for more than 50 years

a widened paved area and a two-way cycle track and a single row of deciduous trees. A second stretch, including the Sauchiehall Precinct, to the east of Sauchiehall Avenue, is due to begin on site in summer 2020.

Scott Parsons, director of strategy and marketing at GSA, is a fan: "The Avenues are quite interesting but they're not about trying to create sterile environments, they're keen on creating active and dynamic environments that still retain what is interesting about this place." What will benefit the Sauchiehall Street and Garnethill area, he says, is the connectivity the Avenues will create, tying

Denim fixing service in COLAB in the Savoy Centre, Glasgow's oldest indoor market. Photo: Jessica Cargill Thompson

GSA and Sauchiehall Street to the West End in one direction and the Speirs Locks Creative Quarter (home to the National Theatre of Scotland and Scottish Opera) in the other. "The whole balance of living and working and moving around the city will be shifted in a substantial way over the next five years. And that's quite exciting."

But not everyone is convinced by the public realm 'improvements'. Some independent galleries around Bath Street say the parking restrictions ("£1 for 15 minutes!") deter business ("Our clients need to drive here. We're tearing our hair out. No one buys a painting on a bike.") and are unimpressed by the recent landscaping of the avenue ("They spent £7m on some stupid trees!").

"It's all very well improving the street to increase footfall," says one local business that's seen a significant dip in trade, "but you have to have something for people to walk down to. At the moment, from Hope Street there's nothing. BHS has been closed for a couple of years [a 12-storey office block is planned for the site, with internal demolition already begun] and there's still a hole where the nightclub [Victoria's] used to be."

Overall, glimmers of confidence are returning to this corner of the city centre. Reactivating the upper floors with workspace and homes promises to bring more people, more energy and more paying customers into

the area. But as COLAB and McLellan Works hope to demonstrate, it is going to take more than just filling the spaces; it will be about forming wider partnerships across the city, from the global institutions, through to the local success stories, to the burgeoning new talent. It will require connectivity – physically via the schemes such as the Avenues, and commercially through networks of entrepreneurs and profit-sharing contracts. And, most importantly, it will need a fine balance of blue-sky thinking and sensitivity to local residents and existing traders to leverage the area's diversity and ensure inclusive growth that doesn't disrupt or displace what is already here.

Find out more
glasgow.gov.uk/avenues

Success in placemaking, whether with the high street or the business park, always requires a tailored, bespoke approach

The Activate – Workman Placemaking team creates commercially viable solutions that add real value to communities, landlords and retailers

Repurposing void retail space is vital in today's challenging retail climate. Nearly 12% of the UK's retail sites were unoccupied in the first half of this year, according to research by the Local Data Company. Despite this gloomy statistic, this is an exciting opportunity for independent retail and leisure operators that can provide a point of difference to outmoded chain stores.

In response, Activate – Workman Placemaking has been launched, bringing together an experienced team of retail and mixed-use development consultants to integrate with Workman's established property management and building consultancy services.

Activate is already engaged on several projects across Workman's portfolio of managed properties and for new clients. We help clients to meet specific asset management objectives, including maximising occupancy levels, supporting occupier retention, increasing footfall, strengthening connections with the local community, and devising meanwhile use interventions. These are often key when changing perceptions and testing new commercial opportunities.

Talking about the service provided, Andrew Sparrow, director at Activate, says: "Placemaking is widely acknowledged as an important element when creating a commercially viable place, whether that be an office, business park or retail location. By putting the users at the centre of the planning, design and management of a space, it strengthens their connections with the place and therefore its value."

One new client which has benefited from our experience is St Helens Council. Like an increasing number of local authorities, the council had purchased several properties in the town centre and wanted support and advice on the development and delivery of a

regeneration strategy, including options for the future of St Mary's Market.

The first step in the project was to understand the views of local residents, stakeholders and market tenants regarding future market provision, leading to an evaluation of the alternative options. We have since followed this with a deeper analysis of the costs and forecast income associated with relocating the market into a void unit in the town.

Working with building consultancy colleagues, Activate has created a new vision for the market that combines independent retail with a food and beverage hub, providing an important business incubator for local entrepreneurs.

Benefiting from more prominent frontage and improved access links, the market will also help to revitalise the town centre, and positively affect surrounding local businesses.

We will continue working with St Helens Council over the coming months, with ongoing detailed business planning, regular tenant consultation and operational support.

In addition to the high street, this approach has proven successful when applied to office environments, where the effectiveness of placemaking initiatives to engage office and business park users can be vitally important for companies in attracting talent and for landlords in ensuring that occupiers stay.

Success in placemaking, whether with the high street or the business park, always requires a tailored, bespoke approach, helping us to understand the customers' and occupiers' requirements and how they interact with the space.

Find out more
Visit activateplaces.co.uk, follow us on Instagram @activateplaces or contact the team on 020 7227 6200

Placemaking success at Birmingham Business Park

Music venues are closing but new ones spring up in railway arches, yards and even former toilets Emma Warren finds out how people come together to make places like this work

Invisible Wind Factory in Liverpool used to be an old warehouse but is now a multi-use destination that includes a music venue. Photo: Alamy

There is a guy strolling through the Kazimier Garden in Liverpool, past the bar and the corrugated iron roof punctuated by colourful lightbulbs and bedecked with greenery. It is a popular meeting spot, with communal benches and a tiny 80-capacity venue housed in an old stock room. New blocks of bulk accommodation sit hard against the sides and the back of the garden, rising high into the skyline.

The Kazimier operates in the gaps, quite literally. It was previously a much larger and much-loved DIY venue where you might find three-day improvised comedy marathons, grassroots music, or purposefully LGBTQ+ friendly late nights alongside touring big names. The land was sold to developer Elliot Group – hence the flats – and it closed on New Year's Day 2016. An abandoned plot of land out the back became the Kazimier Garden.

"It's a very strange sensation to miss a building, to not be able to stand in a particular spot, because it's been demolished," says George Maund, who started out working behind the bar and went on to programme events at The Kazimier. "I can go to my childhood home, if I want to, because that still exists. Without getting overly sentimental about it, it really did hold a unique position in the city," he says.

"It was defined by an octagonal dancefloor, a stage and a balcony, nooks and crannies. You could ambulate the building on the first floor, overlooking what was going on below. You could ornately drape and decorate it. I might have made it sound like any other place that's closed, but perhaps that's the formula right there – for somewhere that means a lot to people.

"What's been lost is ease of access, proximity and a mid-tier 400-ish capacity venue so touring acts can come to Liverpool."

The Kazimier is not alone. In May this year, the International Music Summit published a report showing that 21% of UK nightclubs closed in the year to December 2018 – more than 520 venues. The Music

Total Refreshment Centre in Dalston, central to the London jazz scene, closed in 2018

Venue Trust report that 36% of live music venues had gone by 2016, alongside 18 pubs closing each week in the UK. Viability is less of a problem elsewhere, says the Music Venue Trust: in mainland Europe the average level of government subsidy for grassroots venues is 36% of gross turnover. In France, it is more like 62% as venues are funded to create gathering places and to protect and maintain the French language.

It is not just nightclubs, pubs and venues – it is much of our communal space: The Bureau of Investigative Journalism found that councils have sold 12,000 public spaces since 2014-15 and City Hall reported that more than 100 youth centres closed in the same period. This is relevant: these places helped influential and economically powerful genres like grime germinate. Dizzee Rascal made his musical debut at his local youth club, and you could argue that without London's youth clubs in the early 2000s there would be no Stormzy, with all the money and cultural capital he generates. The Inclosure Acts enacted between 1604 and 1914 took 6.8 million acres of land out of common ownership and it is hard not to see the current scenario as a form of social enclosure.

The discouraging realities around communal space are not stopping a handful of resourceful people making space in the gaps. Take Adam Gerrett and Dom Spillane from Matchstick Piehouse, a people-generated, volunteer-run artspace in a south London railway arch, which offers theatre, burlesque, cabaret, old-school reggae sound system events and the culturally famous Steam Down jams. Upstairs there is a rehearsal room, which you can hire cheaply or in exchange for a shift.

They started running parties and theatre

in a "very dirty" Farringdon arch and were replaced by a wine bar. Relocating to New Cross, they ran events in a community centre where they met sculptors, musicians, and drag artists, all of whom were struggling to find space. They decided to set up a co-operative to support different types of art. "We wanted different people from different art forms supporting each other, and taking communal responsibility for the building," says Gerrett.

A realisation descended: if they ran enough events they could cover the rent, even though rent was inexplicably extortionate everywhere. They located a semi-derelict arch and spent six months rebuilding it, using the carpentry and DIY skills within their community and scrupulously addressed their official and legal responsibilities by reading up on regulation and legislation without spending huge sums on consultants.

"One of the reasons spaces are inaccessible is because people don't think they can do it," says Gerrett. "I discovered that you can do stuff legitimately and DIY. All the boring, lame shit that has to be done – licensing or fire restrictions – can be found online. You can take responsibility."

Theirs is a seriously bare-bones operation. They opened with two loans in July 2018 and ran an event every day for three months to make enough money for the next quarter's rent. The pair put in 70 to 100 unpaid hours a week alongside jobs tutoring and working as life models, working with 30 volunteers. Collectively, they have to bring in around £200 each day, five days a week. "Progress is deeply dependent on free labour. We want to create a system that benefits people and ultimately pays us, but that feels unbelievably far away," says Gerrett.

Like many people who take on the physical and emotional labour of making space, Gerrett's voice contains a backnote of bitterness alongside his clear joy at having created something so valuable. "If you want the control, take some of the responsibility. More artists should be asking these questions and collaborating." The existing systems, he says drily, are not working.

Much of what happens at Matchstick Piehouse is recognisable to Mark Davyd, venue owner and head of the Music Venue Trust, which advocates for the nation's small-scale musical powerhouses. "This entire circuit is built on people identifying a gap locally, filling that gap with whatever is available, then finding ways to keep it going despite the lack of any kind of commercial return," he says. "People who run grassroots venues are extremely inventive. It's written into their DNA. Right from the outset, they'll be thinking about how they can be viable,

"We were previously producing two or three multimillion-pound-selling festival-headliners every year, but we're not producing that any more. We're starting to see a long-term economic and employment impact"

Communal centres such as youth clubs are on the decline. Grime artist Stormzy started his career at one of these venues. Photo: Getty

Steam down jams at Buster Mantis in south London, a similar vibe to the nights put on nearby at Matchstick Piehouse. Photo: George Nelson

The Science of the Lamps perform in the 80-capacity Kazimier Garden in 2013. It used to be part of the 400-capacity Kazimier, which was sold to a developer. Photo: Alamy

even when it's not really viable."

Venues matter, he says, because of the cultural and social aspect. "Interacting through digital space doesn't have the same long-term health, social and networking benefits. It's the Stone Age camp fire, isn't it? Having a place where people can gather, communicate with each other, is fundamentally important. It's difficult to monetise something like that."

It is not easy to make these arguments when people are obsessed with finance. Davyd says that it is easier to quote the simplistic figures: that for every £10 spent in a grassroots music venue, £17 is being spent elsewhere on the broader night-time economy as people buy kebabs or take taxis.

The Music Venue Trust's 550 members include venues that are based in boats (Thekla in Bristol), the end of a terrace (The Adelphi Club in Hull) and a toilet (Davyd's own Tunbridge Wells Forum). "The creative industries are very inventive. It's the other side that lacks imagination. A music venue has negative connotations to developers. You tend to talk about the noise, people causing mess, people who want to smoke outside. Our members are incredibly inventive."

In Bristol, four promoters have managed the almost impossible: crowdfunding £45,000 for a new venue, Strange Brew, and getting the relevant permissions. Like the crew at Matchstick Piehouse, Kerry Patterson and her co-promoters are making space in between full-time jobs: in her case, homelessness prevention.

Their collective, named Dirtytalk, has been running parties and events in the city for nine years. They estimate that 20% of licensed venues have closed in the past seven years, equivalent to 10,000-capacity-worth of bars, venues and clubs. So for the past three years they've been looking for their

own venue. They had previously operated from the Motorcycle Showrooms, a place run on peppercorn rent where they built a bar, a stage and a DJ booth and which has since gone the way of many venues – closed down, awaiting redevelopment. "We wanted to put roots down, so it wasn't so precarious," she says. "We wanted to create a venue that could be lots of different things. There's less and less space, and the space that does exist is being taken over to make way for more flats. Space for the public, or for entertainment or culture is shrinking. I'm feeling hemmed in."

A big factor affecting creative spaces in Bristol is student accommodation, she says, and the relaxation of planning laws allowing developers to turn office buildings into flats without going through the usual hoops. "Student flats are not subjected to the same regulations as other residential buildings so it is a no-brainer – an easy way to acquire buildings for developers for maximum profit."

It sounds like simple stockpiling: many of the new residential buildings, says Patterson, are bought by companies registered in tax havens. Popular venue Blue Mountain in Stokes Croft is about to close and be redeveloped into student accommodation, while legendary venue Motion is under serious threat from two major developments. Pre-austerity, the council had a 'meanwhile project' which matched groups of artists with empty buildings for peppercorn rent. "When poverty hits," adds Patterson, "culture and creative are the first things to go."

The obstacles are replicated country-wide. Back in 2015 the Music Venue Trust was commissioned to write a report for the mayor of London. It listed 22 reasons for the decline, including gentrification, land value, police cuts and issues with licensing and planning permission. "There's one factor that's often cited that I just don't believe,"

says Davyd. "Which is that people aren't interested in seeing live music."

Having slogged its way over the initial hurdles of funding, licensing and planning permission, Dirtytalk is now getting the venue built. "It's been empty for nearly 10 years and it's never been a venue. There are dead rats, crap to clear out. We need to do the plumbing, the toilets, literally everything. We're going to do it properly, but it's not going to be polished. If you can have a wee, have a drink, and if there's a sound system, we'll open," says Patterson.

All things being equal, Bristol will have a new venue that will allow grassroots culture to develop and will provide a space for people to gather. It is a small ray of light amid a much darker picture. The Music Venue Trust is already seeing the economic impact of music venue losses. "We [the UK] were previously producing two or three multimillion-pound-selling festival-headliners every year, but we're not producing that any more. We're starting to see a long-term economic and employment impact," says Davyd.

Back in Liverpool, the Kazimier's George Maund is cautiously optimistic about keeping the garden going, even with the spectre of noise-phobic new arrivals moving in above and around their venue. "We're survivalist adapters. [We'll be here for] another 10 to 15 years, if not longer. I left for two weeks and a fancy bar opened opposite, and a weird quasi-apart-hotel turned its ground floor into a bar, so the area is going to see more of this stacked approach to use of space."

They have evolved into a larger operation, with Invisible Wind Factory, in Liverpool's North Docks, taking over an old warehouse to generate three venues, multiple studio spaces, a workshop for in-house builds and commissions, a tech lab "where lighting arrays and other vibe ideas are tested", and office space. Maund is proud of what he and the team have achieved: "It's a remarkable turnaround from doing a lot with a little.

"Without sounding like I'm justifying gentrification," he says, "when people have to operate in the margins, they do get shit done – on their own terms, almost undisturbed."

It is a lot of work, so why are these resourceful people bothering? "We feel there's no other option," says Patterson. "When you have nowhere to congregate, you're at risk of losing people and talent – the things that make a city interesting. I feel like we can do it. It is possible."

Emma Warren is a journalist and author of Make Some Space, a manifesto for creating musical communities in the 21st century

Entries now open

The Pineapples celebrate the best places in the UK and recognise design excellence and contribution to urban life.

Submit your entry for:

* A completed place
* Place in progress
* Future place
* A project that contributes to place

The P*ineapples

Awards for place

"Great new award... well thought-through judging"
Honor Fishburn, director of placemaking,
Battersea Power Station

2020 timeline

November 2019: call for entries open

February 2020: call for entries deadline

April 2020: finalists announced (published in *The Developer* magazine)

May – June 2020: judges' visits

7 July 2020: finalists present live at the Festival of Place, Tobacco Dock

For more information visit:
www.thepineapples.co.uk

Tripping the light fantastic

Imagine a building filled with light, but with no need for blinds or intensive air conditioning. Merck has made it a reality with its groundbreaking smart glass, creating eyrise™ Dynamic Liquid Crystal Windows

Humans need natural daylight – it is a fundamental part of our biology. Exposure to natural light has a whole host of health benefits, from promoting better sleep to improving our moods. Daylight supports the regulation of vitamin D, serotonin and melatonin in our bodies and promotes healthy eye development[1].

Yet many of us now spend most of our day indoors, moving between our homes and offices. Modern architectural design has already begun to recognise the importance of letting natural light back into our lives, using glass in new and exciting ways. Large, often floor-to-ceiling windows help to bring in a feeling of the outside and of greater space.

However, while this helps to create light-filled buildings, it can also increase building temperatures and personal discomfort for those sitting in direct sunlight.

In particular, the need in offices to reduce glare on screens, control room temperatures or create private meeting spaces means we're still using blinds and partitions – we're shutting ourselves away from the outdoors and natural light.

Increased temperatures also create more demand for air conditioning, while the use of window blinds means relying on additional artificial light. All of this can considerably increase a building's energy usage and environmental footprint.

Yet the business benefits of exposure to natural light are clear: office workers who sit near windows sleep on average for 46 minutes longer at night than those who don't[2], while workplaces with good levels of natural light benefit from productivity gains of up to 40%[1].

This poses the question: how do we balance our need for natural light with the practical and environmental considerations of modern buildings?

You're probably already familiar with liquid crystals. They are used in everything from mobile phones and televisions to microwave ovens and alarm clocks. They are best known for being used in LCDs – liquid crystal displays.

Yet liquid crystals have far wider applications. Merck has been working with them for more than 100 years – almost since their first discovery in 1888 – and our latest solutions have the potential to revolutionise the way we live and work.

"We've taken the technology from LCDs and made it more durable and more robust, so that we can use it in applications such as smart windows," says Dr Ties De Jong, head of technology development for Merck's eyrise™ liquid crystal windows team[4].

The team, based in Veldhoven in the Netherlands, has developed intelligent glass that adapts to light conditions, creating instantly neutral-grey shading and temperature regulation. This is called 'lightwellness' – an always comfortable environment that preserves natural light and outside views.

It has also developed privacy glass, which can be used to create adaptive screening, allowing open, light-filled offices and homes to adapt to the inhabitants' needs for private spaces without losing natural daylight.

This technology has set unprecedented standards for the use of smart glass in architecture. Not only does it enable architects to create buildings that promote

Did you know?

Up to 40%: Workplaces with good levels of natural light benefit from productivity gains of up to 40%

~90%: We spend 80% to 90% of our time indoors[3]

1 second: eyrise™ Dynamic Liquid Crystal Windows can provide shading or privacy screening in just one second

[1] www.eco-business.com/opinion/why-natural-light-matters-in-the-workplace/

[2] www.worldgbc.org/better-places-people/green-healthy-work-spaces

[3] www.researchgate.net/publication/283459751_The_importance_of_light_to_health_and_well-being

[4] www.eyrise.com/about-us/

Smart windows create a comfortable environment that preserves natural light

well-being through natural lighting and outdoor views, it also gives them an important tool for accomplishing their creative vision by offering a whole range of shapes, sizes and colours.

Merck's eyrise™ Instant Solar Shading windows contain a transparent liquid crystal mixture with dye molecules that can be neutral grey or tailored to colour needs. This mixture is placed between two glass sheets coated with a transparent conductive film.

At the flick of a switch, a low voltage causes the liquid crystals to instantly change their orientation, darkening the glass' tint to reduce the amount of light and heat passing through.

However, the windows always remain transparent, so even when darkened, the windows allow natural light to pass through and the outside view is retained. The shading intensity can even be increased or decreased

> "As displays gain more and more space, and as the interfaces between people and information continue to develop, we can envision a future where windows are not just for letting in light or creating privacy, but have information and content displayed on them, too"

to fit with occupants' needs at each and every moment.

Merck's switchable privacy glass works in a similar way, this time using mixtures of cholesteric liquid crystals placed between glass sheets. These respond to a low voltage to turn a truly transparent window into one that is strongly light-scattering.

This adds an opalescent effect to the glass, which is no longer transparent, providing confidentiality on demand with the benefits of daylight.

The first large commercial architectural projects using eyrise™ Dynamic Liquid Crystal Windows are already under way. These include one of the last works of renowned Brazilian architect Oscar Niemeyer – the Niemeyer Sphere, located at crane manufacturer Kirow's headquarters in Leipzig, Germany.

Meanwhile, building firm FC-Gruppe's new headquarters in Karlsruhe, Germany, will become the first structure to use liquid crystal windows across its whole facade.

But the use of liquid crystals in intelligent window glass also opens up exciting technological possibilities for the future.

"Our smart glass is changing the way people interact with the spaces in which they live and work," says Dr Michael Grund, head of business field liquid crystal windows at Merck.

"As displays gain more and more space, and as the interfaces between people and information continue to develop, we can envision a future where windows are not just for letting in light or creating privacy, but have information and content displayed on them, too."

Placetest: MediaCityUK

What is it like to live and work in Peel's 'Media Hub of the North' and has it brought the promised benefits to the deprived areas surrounding it? This exclusive report by anthropologist Rebecca Toop explores the user experience of MediaCityUK, with photography by John Sturrock

Families visit MediaCityUK with their children

Masterplan for the MediaCityUK site, in
collaboration with architect Chapman Taylor:
1 Surface car park
2 Tomorrow workspace and hotel
3 Manchester Ship Canal
4 ITV *Coronation Street* studio
5 Plots C1 and D1, residential
6 MSCP, retail and energy centre
7 Bridge House – BBC offices and residential
8 Peel and BBC studios, office space and hotel
9 Quay House – BBC offices
10 Plot D3, MSCP and residential
11 Plot C3, offices and landscaped park
12 Dock House – BBC offices and residential
13 Public plaza and events space
14 Broadway and link to M60
15 Plot D4, MSCP, offices and energy centre
16 Plot C4, residential and live/work
17 Orange ITV, University of Salford and
office space (built in phase 1)
18 Landscaped park and amenities
19 MediaCityUK Metrolink tram stop
20 Plot D5, residential, retail and car park
21 Plot C5, artisan market
22 Plot C6, residential and retail
23 Plot B5, offices and retail
24 Lowry theatre
25 Broadway Metrolink tram stop
26 Erie Basin
27 Lowry Outlet mall

The offices of the BBC and ITV, as well as the TV studios, make up the core of MediaCityUK

The realisation that the creative class – in this case, media professionals – is an important factor in the regeneration of deprived areas has been influencing policy and development in recent years.

Peel Media's development of MediaCityUK is no exception. Approximately three miles from Manchester city centre and bordered by Eccles, Ordsall, Trafford and Salford, Manchester dockyards remained a brownfield site from their closure in 1982 until Peel began regenerating the area in 2007 as the 'Media Hub of the North'.

There is no question MediaCityUK's design was influenced by the need to provide spaces for broadcasters. Besides the state-of-the-art studios that attracted the BBC as an anchor tenant, Peel has designed the open piazza to accommodate live audiences, who come for shows such as *The Voice* or *BBC Sports Personality of the Year*.

BBC Breakfast sometimes broadcasts from the piazza and shows such as *Blue Peter* often film in the gardens when the weather is good. The big screens in the piazza display BBC content on one side, ITV content on the other, with live sports showings quite well attended in good weather – the deckchairs in the gardens are popular on match days. The big screen is also used to promote MediaCityUK as a brand, with the weekly *Your MediaCity* showcasing the work that is undertaken around the site.

Officially, MediaCityUK contains office blocks that house the BBC, ITV and other companies. It also includes

Looking across North Bay to the Imperial War Museum

studios, apartments, a hotel, a gym, a small supermarket, The Lowry Outlet mall and The Lowry theatre and gallery complex, as well as multiple cafes and restaurants.

But the boundaries of the development vary depending on whom you talk to. People who live and work in MediaCityUK often restrict it to just the side of the development that contains the media: the BBC, ITV, Dock House and so on. They do not include the area across the water that features the outlet mall and gallery.

However, the boundary can also expand to include areas that are not officially part of the development, as many peripheral businesses are attaching the MediaCityUK tag to their premises.

Despite the red lines around the development being fluid in people's minds, the actual design is inward-looking and innately exclusionary, with the buildings arranged in a semi-circle looking down upon the open spaces.

Peel has created what Dan Sodergren, head of business services at MediaCityUK technology incubator The Landing calls a "billion-dollar backdrop. It's an astounding piece of real estate, but you have to go across the river to look back at it... I want to bring the investors in by river next time".

The back of the development varies from the plain and industrial to the downright foreboding – the wall bordering ITV's studios is blank, high, and dotted with CCTV cameras. "They keep themselves very private over there, for obvious reasons," says Sodergren.

In fact, the way in which you access MediaCityUK greatly influences your impression of the area. Those who drive

in go around the outskirts of the site and will be more aware they have arrived in a private, commercial centre, with expensive multi-storey parking. Arriving by public transport drops you in the heart of the development, among the gardens and open space designed to feel like public space, making MediaCityUK very much a destination "at the end of the line".

Cycling is a popular method of getting to work in MediaCityUK. It is not uncommon to see a fold-up bike tucked under someone's desk and there's a well-used bike storage hub on site.

Although some cycle routes to the site are badly designed, others are well maintained, often taking you along the canals. This makes MediaCityUK feel connected to the surrounding areas.

The rise of Generation Z can be felt in MediaCityUK, with social media an important way for Peel to connect to its audience. Josie Cahill, head of stakeholder engagement at Peel, says greater focus on social value for that audience means "the lines between work, play and living are blurring a lot more".

Apartments form the top half of buildings, while studios and offices are on the lower floors. However, this doesn't seem to have led to as much blurring of the two as envisioned.

Opinions of those on the site ranged from, "I think if I didn't work here, I'd want to live here," to, "I think it's a bit weird to have an apartment right next to the BBC. Imagine waking up in the morning and you've got some office man staring at you."

A contributing factor to people not wanting to live and work in MediaCityUK could be the lack of amenities on site. One worker says: "You can't run errands in your lunch break. If I want something from a pharmacy, I have to get my wife to pick it up for me as I don't have time to get there and back during working hours."

As well as no pharmacy, there is no post office, no bank and no large supermarket within a half-hour walk. The Booths on site – the "Waitrose of the North" or "Tory Tesco" – is not the kind of place for a weekly shop.

"It's a sort of grab-and-go or topping-up-a-meal-with-nice-things kind of shop."

There is a gym on site, but membership is £56 a month, compared to £15.99 at a local gym.

Residents' meetings have made Peel aware of the need for more amenities, so this may be changing with the next phase of development. However, Peel says there are challenges to getting these amenities on site.

In general, the fact that MediaCityUK "feels like a campus" is extolled as a virtue: "There's a bubble over MediaCity."

"A contributing factor to people not wanting to live and work in MediaCityUK could be the lack of amenities on site. One worker says: 'You can't run errands in your lunch break. If I want something from a pharmacy, I have to get my wife to pick it up for me as I don't have time to get there and back during working hours.' As well as no pharmacy, there is no post office, no bank and no large supermarket within a half-hour walk"

The University of Salford has a base at the heart of MediaCityUK

The bridge over the Manchester Ship Canal links the Imperial War Museum with MediaCityUK

Manchester United fans drinking in a pub near the Lowry Outlet mall

A walkway between North Bay and Huron Basin links the television studios and offices with the mall

Women born in the 1950s protest about their pensions being underpaid

Cars' access is restricted, so children can play more freely in the area

Summer Weekender was Peel's first 'owned event'

The gardens at the centre of the MediaCityUK semi-circle

Cricket fans walking on Trafford Wharf Road to see a match at Old Trafford cricket ground

The area around MediaCityUK was formerly an area of considerable industrial activity

However, it has fallen into decline and parts of it are considerably deprived

The canals enable activities that would be impossible on other developments

Arriving by public transport drops you in the heart of the development

Fans of England fast bowler Jofra Archer on their way to watch the Ashes Test match at Old Trafford

Geese and gulls are frequent visitors to the area, but they rarely nest as there is little greenery on the water's edge

In the shade of the Lowry theatre

Local children from Eccles swimming in Huron Basin

The bridge by The Lowry gallery complex connects MediaCityUK to the Manchester United stadium at Old Trafford

MediaCityUK is the start and finish point of the UKFast City of Salford 10k road race

The lines between work, play and living are blurring on the development

The monthly Makers Market offers local food, drink, art and design

The Lowry theatre and gallery complex

Like a campus, there are sports clubs, triathlons, basketball courts and football pitches that are free to book if you are a resident or work in the buildings. There are also regular freebies, including free magazines available in the buildings, drinks giveaways and ice-cream promotions.

There is certainly the feeling that once you live or work in MediaCityUK, perks open up to you. Whether or not these perks encourage people to buy into the brand, there are many people who work here who consider themselves part of MediaCityUK. They use the pronoun 'we' to mean 'people who work in MediaCityUK', rather than just people who work at the BBC or ITV.

The social capital that MediaCityUK provides gives people a collective identity. "All the sport comes from up here as well, so when you see sport on *BBC News* you're like 'Oh, that's us!'"

As Jane Jacobs theorised in *The Death and Life of Great American Cities*, there is often in a city "one spot where politicians gather, one stretch of sidewalk where, if you stand there at noon, you will see everybody in town".

MediaCityUK is built to house the media equivalent on a large scale and there is a sense of being surrounded by media professionals. Snippets of conversation I overhear include the lining up of guests on a radio show. Workers say: "It feels like you're in the middle of things when you see people filming around you"; and "You do get a few people coming here and hoping to catch a glimpse of a VIP when *The Voice* is in."

Onlookers regularly peek into the glass-fronted radio studio when musicians are playing for the morning shows, wanting to be part of the action.

Many people come to MediaCityUK to attend recordings of radio and TV shows

"Buildings are designed as stepping stones: micro and small businesses can start in The Greenhouse, which offers hot-desking and small office spaces, then move their way up through the Tomorrow building to many of the more well-established towers such as White or Blue. Being on the same site as the BBC and having access to shared facilities, as well as 5G broadband, cannot hurt a business either"

Henrietta Rowlatt, an assistant producer at 7digital and BBC 6 Music, says: "You feel a bit like an animal in a zoo because they are all looking at you."

There are regular tours around the buildings and into the studios, and it feels like a theme park for the public has been created, with the media hub as the main attraction.

"It's a tourist destination, ain't it?" says Rowlatt.

So how does it feel to have people coming to your place of work for recreation?

Jack, a BBC employee, says: "I think it's quite cool. It's like, 'Oh yeah, I work here, and you want to have a little glimpse into my life.'"

Rowlatt adds: "It's a bit surreal. It's one of the most surreal places I've ever worked. When I come to work on Friday and Saturday, there are all these people running past me, soaking wet, going to jump on an obstacle course, and they look like gladiators. This is a really weird place to work."

As well as all the opportunities given to the public to feel more involved in the media they consume, there is a strong atmosphere of opportunities being created for those who work or study within MediaCityUK. The Landing "has helped more than 1,600 people either start their own businesses or make their way into work", according to Sodergren.

Buildings are designed as stepping stones: micro and small businesses can start in The Greenhouse, which offers hot-desking and small office spaces, then move their way up through the Tomorrow building to many of the more well-established towers such as

White or Blue. Being on the same site as the BBC and having access to shared facilities, as well as 5G broadband, cannot hurt a business either.

The University of Salford has a base at the heart of MediaCityUK. Rowlatt says: "It must be amazing for those students to work here. You see them walking around with all their kit, filming, and stuff like that. I mean I studied media but it was in Wolverhampton – it's not quite the same as actually studying in MediaCity!"

There is also the University Technical College based just next to MediaCityUK ("it's built there for a reason!"), which aims to pipeline students into The Landing and, from there, get someone like the BBC as a client.

Sodergren says, "There is a huge chasm between the two realities," but Cahill hopes The Landing can bridge that chasm, feeding into the "wider ecosystem" of MediaCityUK as a whole.

Chris Reay, property director at Peel, says: "You've got large corporates that want to be associated with and take on board the ideas and creativity of agile, small companies, and equally, small companies want to be able to work and rub shoulders with big corporates."

The media industry runs on a high level of social networking, much of which is done outside the workplace. People will regularly hold meetings in the bars and cafes, and Social 7 is MediaCityUK's version of a business lounge.

Sodergren says: "I think there's a presumption that a culture of collaboration can instantly exist just because of the potential. What's exciting about here is that the potential is so huge that I think that would bring everyone close together anyway."

But rather than just setting up the infrastructure to enable this potential, Peel wants to be seen to take an active role, connecting companies with universities, hospitals and other businesses. Reay says: "We can facilitate that as the manager of the whole environment."

But what Cahill calls this "long-term custodianship role of the site" has its drawbacks. Despite all the talk of MediaCityUK being an ecosystem, it feels anything but organic. People do sit and read books on the children's play equipment and occasionally nap on benches; the green space is used for eating lunches and walking dogs. But use of the space is still largely prescribed – MediaCityUK is not the kind of place you would bring a barbecue and you don't see kids on skateboards. This may be due to the constant security presence, with guards frequently visible riding around on Segways ("Am I in *Robocop* or something?" asks Rowlatt). It could also be because the outdoor spaces are largely exposed and feel overlooked – there are few tucked-away spaces that give any privacy from the office blocks and studios.

"They seem to not want people there… It seems odd. You can kind of see how it's designed in a way where it would stop people doing certain stuff," says one worker.

Large areas of the development are open space with very little greenery at all, although the council is working on the part of the development it owns, between The Lowry and the Lowry Outlet, as part of a project aptly named 'Greening the Grey'.

The Lowry Outlet came under Peel's ownership in 2012. "That is why we bought it – to take control, basically," says Reay.

However, it still feels very separate, both geographically and in terms of the audience it attracts. Rowlatt says: "The Lowry Outlet feels a bit depressing sometimes. I don't tend to go there. It's not great. The broken biscuit chocolate shop is good! Go to that one but ignore the rest."

But with Peel's repositioning of the site, it is unclear whether it will improve its offering while appealing to the same demographic that it currently enjoys or homogenise it to fit with the rest of the development.

"You've got that little bit of snobbishness… I don't think they thought Greggs would attract the right sort of people," says a worker.

Instead of curating your audience, a good development should create an atmosphere. One worker describes this as being where "everyone's invited and everyone can come and have a play and everyone can enjoy it. Now, OK, maybe not a skate ramp – maybe that's a bit too street – but certainly there are things that you could do to help that."

Another cautions: "I think there's a danger if you just go for a certain demographic, it could become something you don't want it to be."

But what do locals think of MediaCityUK?

"When the BBC first moved in, there was a sense that clearly this is quite a deprived area whwere we were building this brilliant shiny new development. The BBC, for every single event or production or show, always ringfence at least 25% of their tickets to local, Salford postcodes"

Security staff travel on Segways

Buggies lined up in the window of the Lowry theatre during a children's show

Adam, a local resident, says: "Salford's reputation has not been great, but [MediaCityUK] has had an impact on the local area. It's nice to hear that little spots where it used to be really bad – that whole area with the upside-down houses used to not be a nice area to go in – because of this development, there are a lot of professionals who want to live there, which makes the area safe. It gentrifies the area. So from my point of view, I'm thankful that this has happened."

Attracting a 'new urban elite' to improve an area is one thing, but Arie Romein, Jeannette Nijkamp and Jan Jacob Trip argued in *Creativity-Led Regeneration: Towards An Evaluation Framework* that there should be a move towards strengthening the cultural identity of an area "in a way that the resident population feels at home".

The site's cultural history as a dockyard is venerated in a sculpture walk. This features quotes from residents ("Oranges and chocolates were thrown from the Manchester liners coming through the canal" – Pauline Thompson, Dock 9 sculpture); poetry ("Don't snub your nose at history, the future lives on the past of folks like we" – Centenary Walkway); and mosaics and engravings by local children imagining the places from which exotic goods arrived in Salford.

Sadly, these links to the past are not prominent in the landscape and are not well kept. The quotes, although engraved, are

losing their colour, making them difficult to read, and the mosaics are losing their tiles. Perhaps maintaining the links to Salford's working-class past is no longer a priority.

Despite some locals' concerns that "areas such as Eccles that need development have this development on their doorstep that's not for them" and fears that if "it doesn't look like them" then the development will alienate some people, there is certainly an effort being made to engage with local audiences.

Cahill says: "When the BBC first moved in, there was a sense that clearly this is quite a deprived area where we were building this brilliant shiny new development. The BBC, for every single event or production or show, they always ringfence at least 25% of their tickets to local, Salford postcodes."

The BBC also runs a 'Young Ambassadors' scheme that gets local young people into paid work experience placements. Peel also wanted to include local people and businesses right from the construction stage. Reay says: "When we constructed the BBC buildings, 12% of workers on site were from Salford and 51% from Greater Manchester. We delivered 220 apprenticeships to local people through just that three-year period of construction."

Peel has done well to attract families to MediaCityUK – the fact that cars are restricted on the site means that children can run around more freely.

Rowlatt says: "You see families coming here and having picnics, all walks of life, everyone just chilling out on the grass, which is really, really lovely to see."

It also feels very safe. Security on site is largely a "customer service-driven role, mostly because there's not really too much going on around MediaCity", according to Josh, a member of MediaCityUK's security. Even on busy match days, where its proximity to Old Trafford is keenly felt, there has never been any trouble.

Reay says: "We try to use the public realm as much as possible to create a place that the local residents want to use at the weekend or in their spare time."

Peel has just had what Cahill calls its first "owned event" – the Summer Weekender, featuring music, craft activities, funfair rides and food. She says the company concentrated on accessibility and keeping the cost to attend "as low as humanly possible", with tickets costing £4 and under-threes getting free entry.

There have been other festival-style events, too, which Adam says "we have never really had locally". Recently, Architects of Air built on the piazza a 5m-long inflatable structure, 'Arboria Luminarium', that was free to enter.

Gabriel Burden, manager at the luminarium, says: "The visitors have been from lots of different backgrounds. It's a real cross-section, which is great. I thought it would be very media types and officey types. But actually it's not."

But how accessible is it to put on an event in MediaCityUK? There was a feeling among some of the independent organisations and smaller businesses based at MediaCityUK that Peel "charges an extortionate amount of money for putting on events", to the point where small-to-medium businesses are limited to holding events in the bars and communal office spaces.

Cahill says: "We have an arrangement with the BBC, for example, where they get a certain quota of free space a year, because we want to encourage them [to put on events] and because they're publicly funded... similarly charities and things."

But how diverse is Peel willing to be? She says: "It would just need to fit with what our vision and values are for the space... I think if you mix in too many different types of events, people are confused about what the place is about. But diversity is obviously really important, based on where we are, so we produce activity that makes sense to local audiences."

Peel has just secured a £292.5m loan for the next phase of MediaCityUK's expansion, the plans for which it is currently drawing up. The company has "smart city ambitions", according to Cahill, and Sodergren believes MediaCityUK is in an enviable position to achieve these ambitions.

"There's only one centralised management system, which is very, very rare," he says, "so it means that smart city stuff can be done very, very rapidly. It's just sitting it on top of the same infrastructure."

There is also the expectation that Peel will be able to tap into the "skills pipeline" of tech companies based on the site. "It most probably won't be the big corporates that will [implement smart initiatives] – it'll be the smaller start-ups that we hopefully helped create at The Landing." Sodergren hopes that what is achieved in MediaCityUK will benefit wider society: Salford and beyond.

Another potential focus for the next phase will be capitalising on MediaCityUK's waterfront position, turning the water into even more of an asset. It currently enables some events to be put on that are outside the norm, such as the Neon night swim, triathlons and dragon-boat competitions (although the latter is not organised by

"The visitors have been from lots of different backgrounds. It's a real cross-section, which is great. I thought it would be very media types and officey types. But actually it's not"

MediaCityUK). River tours can also be taken from the site.

However, there is little sense of life on the water. Birds such as swans and seagulls are frequent visitors, but no nests are visible. There is little greenery on the water's edge, and no houseboats moor up along this stretch of the canals.

Reay says: "We've got some fairly wacky ideas about what we'd like to use [the water] for, on a consumer basis."

It will be interesting to see if Peel can give the water a life of its own or whether it becomes a branded, commercial asset for MediaCityUK.

The ongoing 'custodianship' that Peel has over MediaCityUK has the potential to mean far more can be achieved in the space. Its input has obviously been beneficial for those that work here. It has fostered creative talent, with many of the nation's best-loved TV shows being produced here. It has actively maintained a network of tech start-ups and big media companies through networking events and opportunities to socialise outside work. Engagement with locals has also been proactive.

However, there may be a need to host a broader range of events and to empower local people by allowing them to use the space less formulaically, in ways with which they are comfortable.

It has been said that MediaCityUK "lacks authenticity" and "looks imported". Allowing the use of the 'public realm spaces' to develop more organically and dynamically can only have a positive impact on this.

MediaCityUK job stats
A report by Paul Swinney and Gabriele Piazza for Centre for Cities in 2017 analysed the effect on employment in Greater Manchester of the BBC's relocation to MediaCityUK. It found that the projections had been over-optimistic and that many jobs simply moved from elsewhere in Greater Manchester

Decision to relocate BBC operations to MediaCityUK: 2006
Predicted jobs created: 15,000
Move began: 2011

Net jobs created by 2016: 4,550
Media jobs: +3,900 (2,000 by BBC)
Knowledge intensive based activities: +1,090
Hotel and hospitality: +340
Retail: -350
Other sectors: -430

Jobs created by companies moving from elsewhere in the country: 145
Jobs created by BBC moving Greater Manchester operations: 640
Jobs created by other companies moving from elsewhere in Greater Manchester: 560

Increase in media jobs in Greater Manchester: 72% (from 4,520 to 7,760)

Overall, the BBC's move to Greater Manchester was responsible for 0.3% of all jobs in the region in 2016

Source: www.centreforcities.org/reader/ move-public-sector-jobs-london/ relocation-bbc-activities-salford/

The paradox of the ever and never-changing

Has change become the only constant? CallisonRTKL director **John Badman** reasons with the existential and considers how the human condition can be good for business

We are in rapidly changing, ever evolving times. In fact, the rate of change has never been faster.

Call it the 'law of accelerating returns' or the 'age of accelerations'. Whatever the case, it's disrupting the field of play for all of us. The way we communicate, work, relax, socialise, even date has changed, is still changing and may never stop changing.

Such exponential change requires exponential thinking. But when traditional constructs of value, service and experience are being redefined, where do we start?

Throughout the first, second and now third revolution, there remains an aspect of the human condition that has withstood the test of time – our needs. We can trace all actions and reactions back from here; better yet, we can use them to anticipate behaviour. When little else is certain, that knowledge might just be the anchor we're looking for.

The outlook gets brighter still with these needs already defined for us by psychologist, Abraham Maslow. His 1943 paper, *A Theory of Human Motivation*, captures the universal needs of society and our higher emotional pursuits.

Often depicted as a pyramid, Maslow's 'hierarchy of needs' can be understood in three sections. The first layers comprise physiological and safety needs, those pertinent to our survival such as food, water, warmth, rest, safety and security. The next layers focus on psychological needs relating to belonging, love and esteem, while the final layer concentrates on the need for self-fulfilment.

Predicated on fulfilling innate human needs in priority and culminating in self-actualisation, this theory underpins what we're striving to create in the built environment – places that serve more than our basic needs, places that people love, that support them in reaching their full potential.

How do we deliver this? Tech's Big Four certainly seem to have the answers. Google, Amazon, Facebook and Apple have all succeeded, tapping into our higher needs and feeding our desire for connection, acceptance and discovery.

They have created places for people to meet and connect, to be seen and heard, to be praised and entertained, in much the same way we seek to. And while their communities are digital and their marketplaces virtual, they have more in common with the models of our ancient cities than we might think.

Take specifically Greek city-states circa 3,000 years ago, where the concept of the 'agora' was born. The original 'gathering place' or 'assembly' as it is literally translated, the agora was the heart of athletic, artistic, spiritual and political life. Homes were built around it, with citizens and consumers alike coming together while merchants traded from stalls and artisans whittled away in nearby workshops.

The agora created a seamless lifestyle experience that took the friction, time, effort and drudgery out of daily life – an effect our tech giants are seeking to replicate in the digital sphere, while we do so in the physical realm.

The parallels between old and new worlds suggest that we may not have changed as much as we think. Our lifestyle ecosystems are certainly more diverse and globalised in a digital age, but the ethos hasn't been lost. We're still living, working, shopping and socialising – it's just the ways in which we are doing so that have changed. The acts themselves haven't and, really, nor have we.

We share meals just as the cavemen once did. We form tribes. We hunt and gather (albeit fewer woolly mammoths and more bargains).

Deep down, the needs we are seeking to meet are the same.

We can take great solace in this. Apply it to seemingly insurmountable questions like, "What do future consumers, future residents, future employees, want?" and the answer becomes more easily understood. People want what they've always wanted –

"The parallels between old and new worlds suggest that we may not have changed as much as we think. Our lifestyle ecosystems are certainly more diverse and globalised in a digital age, but the ethos hasn't been lost"

John Badman has been at the forefront of the build to rent (BtR) sector since its inception in the UK. Contributing to both editions of the ULI Best Practice BtR Design Guides, he sits across multiple BTR committees and informs the development of lifestyle-led residential investment product.

As a director of CallisonRTKL (CRTKL) John leads the global architecture and design firm's residential team across the UK and Europe. Having shaped more than 8,000 BtR units across the UK, his commercial acumen and human-centric design approach are well documented – as is his ability to bring together cross-sector expertise within the firm to create solutions of increased value

CRTKL's Phase One Station Hill design in Reading for Lincoln MGT

Amenities designed by CRTKL create a sense of community in this build-to-rent scheme

they want community, belonging, fulfilment and cohesion. This should be the blueprint for our future cities.

We are already moving in this direction with contemporary urban fabrics planned more holistically to include intentional overlap between the retail, commercial, hospitality and residential environments. We are even starting to see this pay off, with those employing integrated solutions and incorporating mixed uses also improving their yields, rental returns and occupancy rates.

As our world expands into new dimensions, this is what securing the future of a real estate asset looks like. We need to move beyond placemaking and into human-centric urbanism. We need to put people at the heart of decision-making. We need to expand our thinking beyond any one front door and give greater consideration to the spaces in between.

This is where the seamless lifestyle experience is created and where we shape the experiences required to fulfil our highest needs.

Within a building, these spaces take the form of amenities. Designed to encourage interaction and foster relationships with the inhabitants, amenities take many forms, from communal gardens and libraries to wellness centres and rooftop entertaining areas. When done well, the effect is twofold: tenants are happier and returns are higher.

In fact, our research in the build-to-rent and private rented sector shows that residents who know another person in their building are 70% more likely to renew their lease and 90% more likely if they know two or more.

The social and commercial incentives continue when we look beyond a singular building. Taking a more inclusive view of the streetscape and applying the agora model, we find greater opportunities for the collective.

Here, new recreational initiatives can bring renewed interest from residents and workers, with this then increasing footfall for existing retail and hospitality offerings. These initiatives regenerate underused space for public enrichment, with amphitheatres, parks, playgrounds and more offered up as flexible canvases for expression, creativity and entertainment.

These shared places complete our lifestyle ecosystem and bring together all the extra parts and services that make life a little bit more comfortable, convenient and enjoyable. This is where the local favourites are made, from the coffee shop to the bar, the greengrocer to the deli and bakery, the cycle studio to the boutique and arthouse.

Unsurprisingly, this is where most of our dispensable income is spent, which makes sense when we look at this through Maslow's eyes. These extras, these amenities and shared places, directly align with our highest needs. This is what makes the difference between a good neighbourhood and a great one. This is where profits are made or lost.

Herein lies the answer, in times where everything seems to be changing, bank on human nature staying true.

CRTKL is a global consultancy elevating the human experience with architecture, design and technology. Over the past 70 years, the collective strength of its capabilities has created some of the world's most memorable and successful environments for developers, retailers, investors, institutions and public entities. They are a team of creative thinkers who put people at the heart of what they do. CRTKL's local intelligence combines with cross-sector expertise to enhance the world around us

Billions have already been spent on HS2 but it could still be cancelled. This must not happen

The UK's next high-speed rail project was over budget and facing political pressure before it had even broken ground. Conservative voters do not want the Y-shaped network linking London, Birmingham, Manchester and Leeds to pass through their backyards, and conditions are proving more complicated than expected. But Nicole Badstuber suggests that many of HS2's problems are common to other 'megaprojects' around the world – and that despite the issues, it still needs to go ahead

Early works on HS2 in progress in Euston this summer. Photo: HS2

Anne Stevens, vicar of St Pancras Church, chains herself to a tree outside Euston to protest against the planned clearance of the trees in the area to make way for HS2. Photo: Getty

At the publication of the House of Lords' Economic Affairs Committee report, *The Economics of High Speed 2*, the committee's chair, Lord Forsyth of Drumlean, concluded: "The costs of HS2 do not appear to be under control."

The former chair of HS2, Sir Terry Morgan, agrees. "Something will have to give" on the project management triangle of time, cost and scope, he believes. Costs are spiralling upwards and Phase One, which links London and Birmingham, is now nearly five years late. There is therefore concern that the government will cancel Phase Two of the Y-network, which branches north of Birmingham to run to both Manchester and Leeds.

Lord Forsyth warned: "If costs overrun on the first phase of the project, there could be insufficient funding for the rest of the new railway. The northern sections of High Speed 2 must not be sacrificed to make up for overspending on the railway's southern [between London and Birmingham] sections."

The Economic Affairs Committee instead reiterated the cost-saving measures it had recommended in its previous, 2015 report: lowering the speed on the railway or starting it in west London rather than at Euston.

The strategic case for HS2 is based on capacity. The government aims to improve connectivity by providing more services and shorter journey times. The new HS2 network will add railway lines for use by fast, longer-distance services, freeing up capacity on existing rail lines to run more local, regional and commuter services.

Although Phase One will reduce journey times between London and Birmingham, achieving more significant time savings will require the completion of Phase Two. That will cut journey times between London and Manchester from two hours to one, while trips between Birmingham and Newcastle will be reduced from nearly three hours to less than two. Journey times between Manchester and Birmingham will more than halve, dropping from 88 minutes to only 40.

Investment in the HS2 network will improve rail services for both long-distance and local rail users. But it has polarised opinion and anti-HS2 sentiment is striking a chord with politicians. Polling also suggests the new railway is unpopular with the public, particularly Conservative voters.

And so, at the end of August, the government announced an independently led government review into whether and how HS2 should proceed. The review will assess a range of characteristics, including benefits, impacts, affordability, deliverability and construction phasing. The review's final report, which will inform the government's

As Financial Times journalist Gill Plimmer wrote in response to the price hike, "Few expected the costs to spiral out of control before a single metre of track had been laid"

decision about its next steps for the project, is due imminently. In the meantime, limited, largely preparatory work will continue on the project in parallel with the report's work.

Projected costs for HS2 have ballooned. The government announced in September that the estimated price tag had soared by £26bn to £88bn – a 41% cost increase on previously published numbers. Political and financial problems have plagued the new railway line, initially sold as an alternative to expanding London's Heathrow Airport and as an extension of the existing HS1 high-speed rail link to Europe. However, the current plans do not directly connect HS2 to either.

Deadlines for running services have also been blown apart. Trains were due to start running between London and Birmingham in 2026, but that date has been revised back to 2028-2031. They also will not initially run to the city centre termini of London Euston and Birmingham New Street but to London Old Oak Common and Birmingham Curzon Street. Services on the two branches north of Birmingham are also delayed at least five years and are now due in 2038-2040, instead of late 2033. Phase Two itself is uncertain, as it requires parliament to pass legislation, which is not planned until 2023.

Building the fastest railway in the world, with two-thirds of the route from London to Birmingham in tunnels, was always an ambitious feat of engineering. But as *Financial Times* journalist Gill Plimmer wrote in response to the price hike, "Few expected the costs to spiral out of control before a single metre of track had been laid."

However, there were warning signs that this ambitious 'megaproject' would be significantly over budget and delayed from the start. Across HS2 reporting, the most prominent and frequently quoted cost estimate was £55.7bn for the full network. The origin of this figure – approximately £64.8bn in 2019 prices – can be traced back to the 2013 Spending Review.

Importantly, however, £55.7bn was never the estimated cost of HS2 but how much funding was available for it. The new

£88bn price tag announced in September is therefore the first official estimate in the six years since it was approved. The fact that no official cost estimate has been published in this time has shrouded the project in a veil of murkiness.

There has been no official announcement of cost increases either. However, there have been warning signs. Back in May 2016, the then-chancellor George Osborne warned of soaring project costs. This was a year before parliament legislated for Phase One. The National Audit Office (NAO) also reviewed HS2 in 2016 and found significantly more money than the agreed funding envelope would be needed to complete the full network – £64.9bn (roughly £73.2bn in 2019 prices).

Megaprojects – defined as very large, complex endeavours, typically costing more than US$1bn (£815m) – typically balloon in cost and falter in expectation. In 2011, the NAO reviewed the successful delivery of some 40 major government projects. It found that two-thirds were completed late, over budget or did not deliver the outcomes expected.

Research by Bent Flyvbjerg, professor of major programme management at the University of Oxford's Saïd Business School, discovered even fewer megaprojects delivered their promised benefits, were on time and on budget. Flyvbjerg's database of megaprojects shows that only 10-20% of megaprojects came in on budget, 10-20% were delivered on time and 10-20% demonstrated their promised benefits. The number of projects that delivered on all three criteria was less than 1%.

Earlier research by Aalborg University in Denmark found that for rail megaprojects specifically, actual costs are 45% higher on average than the estimated costs. It also found that a third of rail projects were between 40% and 60% over budget.

These failures may be the result of treating megaprojects as simply large projects scaled up. Megaprojects take many years to develop, plan and build. They involve many stakeholders and are expected to be transformational. Importantly, says Flyvbjerg, they are a "completely different breed of project in terms of their level of aspiration, stakeholder involvement, lead times, complexity and impact". He says this important difference is often missed and conventional project management regimes are applied.

Instead, project managers who are reflective leaders and domain specialists are needed. Often, the delivery of megaprojects involves setting up, running and taking down temporary management organisations the size of billion-pound corporations. The establishment of new organisation and

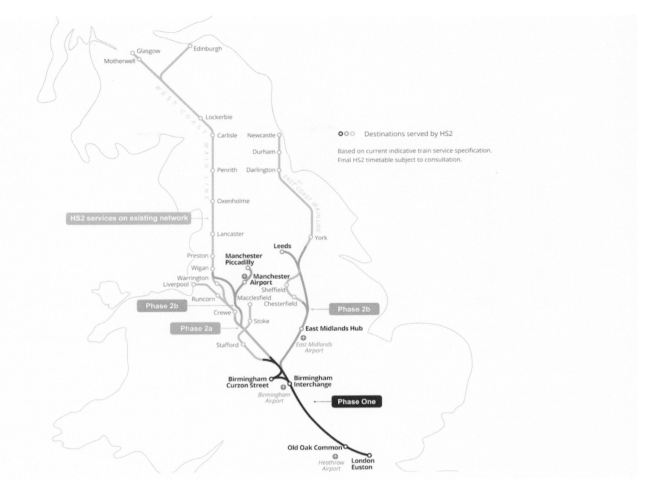

The planned Y-shaped HS2 network

Birmingham's HS2 terminus, Curzon Street

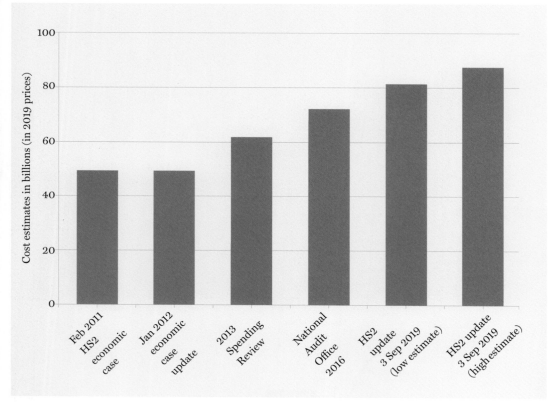

Projected cost estimates for HS2. Sources: House of Commons Library, Department for Transport and National Audit Office

governance structures for these corporations is a staggering feat in its own right.

HS2 demonstrates all the hallmarks of a megaproject and the challenges of managing one, particularly unforeseen complexity leading to cost overruns and project delivery delays. The reasons cited for HS2's cost overruns and delays are the need for an additional tunnel, ground conditions that were more complicated than expected, underestimated land and property values, and poor corporate governance.

To appease disgruntled Conservative voters in the Chiltern Hills area, politicians committed to 50km of tunnels between London and Birmingham – two-thirds of the route. This would involve tunnelling through hundreds of different soil types including

Optimism bias was adversely affecting projects, leading to an over-optimistic view of costs and benefits. It too concluded that the optimism bias was strategically motivated, to increase the likelihood of a project being awarded funding

porous salt mines and chalky rubble. Soft and fine soils will require stabilisation with concrete support structures. These changes added costs to the project.

HS2 has been criticised for insufficiently budgeting for the unknown soil conditions and associated risk to schedule and cost. Criticism is specifically directed at its failure to investigate ground conditions and reliance on available studies. HS2 has defended its actions on the grounds that it "didn't yet have the legal power to access land". Yet, the ramifications of insufficient information about the ground conditions along HS2's route are extensive.

To build Phase One of HS2, the government will need to acquire 70 square kilometres of land. Initially, £3.6bn was budgeted for this and according to the *Financial Times*, 900 homes, farms and properties have so far been bought at a cost of £2.2bn (2019 prices).

However, NAO estimated in 2018 that the cost of purchasing land and property along the route would be higher than that initial figure, as a result of rises in property values and the introduction of additional compensation schemes.

Collectively, megaprojects' persistent underperformance on delivering benefits and their additional costs undermine the value and validity of the methods used to appraise them. Flyvbjerg concludes that the scale of inaccuracy in forecasts suggests that projects are intentionally being put forward with misleading cost estimates. Simply put,

projects are presented in a favourable light to get them approved, thereby misleading politicians and the public about the actual costs of the project.

An NAO review of the delivery of public sector projects supports his view. It found that optimism bias was adversely affecting projects, leading to an over-optimistic view of costs and benefits. It too concluded that the optimism bias was strategically motivated, to increase the likelihood of a project being awarded funding.

Despite their poor record, megaprojects remain a popular endeavour. Flyvbjerg and colleagues have identified four drivers fuelling the development of megaprojects: technological, political, economic and aesthetic. Technological refers to engineers' and technologists' excitement at building the next biggest, tallest and fastest project. Political is politicians' excitement to build a monument to themselves and leave a legacy. Economic is the promise of jobs and business. Finally, aesthetic is the gratification of building good, iconic design.

Arguably, all four are present in the case of HS2: to build the fastest railway in the world, to demonstrate politicians' commitment to infrastructure development, to create new jobs in designing, constructing and running the new railway, and to build Britain's high-speed railway network.

But megaprojects' poor records don't obviate the need for them. The government's own analysis found that capacity issues in the North of England could not be addressed by train improvements and enhancements, and that West Coast Main Line train services were unlikely to improve without major investment. The completion of the full HS2 network will enable more local rail services to be run between cities and towns in the North of England. Crowding and infrequent shorter-distance services are not a problem limited to London and Birmingham. It is imperative that the construction of HS2 is not halted before Phase Two is complete.

Nicole Badstuber is an urban infrastructure researcher at the Centre for Digital Built Britain and University of Cambridge

HS2 works in Euston have already begun. However, cutbacks may require HS2 to start from London Old Oak Common Station instead

Resilient New York

Patricia Brown reports on how successive mayors have tried to make the Big Apple future-fit, leaner, greener and greater in a city that is all about the deal

The bold, partial pedestrianisation of New York's Times Square – the 'Crossroads of the World'

Back in 2012, two urbane, well-prepared New York deputy mayors went head-to-head with a rather shambolic Boris Johnson and his sparring partner. The occasion was a debate I had helped establish to raise money for LandAid, the property industry's charity, to battle out which of these two world cities deserved to be crowned the 'best for business'.

Both cities volleyed on their respective strengths – from policy initiatives and investment, through share of global HQs, to the meteoric rise of innovation and digital industries. But the debate did more to underscore their similarities than points of departure. That London won the audience vote was more down to its home field advantage than a winning argument and masterful debate on the behalf of the city's then-mayor.

Johnson seemed genuinely surprised that his place of birth could be a credible challenge to the city he governed, but I abstained from voting as I felt conflicted, my deep affection for both cities tested.

It has been more than 20 years since my professional relationship with London's twin city first started. Since then, I have pinged back and forth, observing their changes and trading expertise, to help them remain great places to live and work.

Over that time, their populations have grown, economies have risen (and fallen) in parallel, and fast-growing creative and tech ecosystems have helped to rebalance them after the global recession, bringing a very different vibe to the business landscape.

In the late 1990s, when I was CEO of the Central London Partnership (CLP), I sat at the metaphorical knees of New York experts to help us kickstart business improvement districts (BIDs), which had proved a highly effective way of getting business involvement and funds to help New York clean up its act.

New York's urban intensity is an intrinsic part of its character and appeal, but Bloomberg recognised that people were increasingly seeking a softer centre to their urban buzz – clean air, and walking or biking down tree-lined streets to a local park or pedestrian plaza to watch the world go by, work or play with their kids

We used the knowledge of New York's officials and BID leaders to get under the skin of many of the issues we wanted to solve in London, from partnership solutions through policing to the basic mechanics of setting up this new form of urban management in the UK. We saw things that were familiar and transferable, others that were very different.

In one early visit to explore BIDs in operation, Farebrother's Alistair Subba Row hit the nail on the head when he said of New York: "It's all about deals. We need to be able to do deals."

I saw BIDs as a means to an end – part of a wider strategy to up the ante on London's public realm, retrofitting people and urban quality into city planning and pushing quality of life far higher up the agenda. As CLP's work got traction, my New York colleagues looked to London to help with their transport and public space challenges and for tips on getting their city's leaders to address them.

Then came mayor Michael Bloomberg and deputy mayor Dan Doctoroff's PlaNYC – the 2007 strategic plan for a "greener, greater New York". This addressed the twin goals of climate change and quality of life, echoing CLP's mantra that this is the key to retaining talent – the biggest asset of a knowledge economy – and fundamental to a city's economic success.

New York's urban intensity is an intrinsic part of its character and appeal, but Bloomberg recognised that people were increasingly seeking a softer centre to their urban buzz – clean air, and walking or biking down tree-lined streets to a local park or pedestrian plaza to watch the world go by, work or play with their kids.

The administration worked at pace on an audacious roll-out of measurable goals, underpinned by a strong focus on sustainability: a network of pedestrian plazas, family-friendly streets, bike lanes, bike shares, and waterfront and neighbourhood parks, with the aim of providing all New Yorkers with green space no more than a 10-minute stroll away. One part of this was a target of adding one million trees in 10 years.

Probably the most high-profile scheme was Times Square – the 'Crossroads of the World' – where the Times Square Alliance, the BID led by Tim Tompkins, had been struggling with the problems of 'success' caused in part by the clean-up of the district. The area's pavements now had more people than they could handle, so the experience for visitors and workers alike needed to be upgraded to maintain the area's offer.

Some progress had been made, nibbling space from cars to give to people, but despite the alliance's vision and creative approach, it was slow and hard-won.

When transportation commissioner Janette Sadik-Khan first mooted a total pedestrianisation of the 'bow tie' section of Broadway, it was both surprising and bold. To make its introduction more palatable and speedier, the change was proposed as a short-term pilot. But it quickly proved popular and viable, leading to the commission of Snøhetta to design the permanent transformation.

Creating more space for people is only part of the task of sustaining a busy tourist destination that is also a vibrant business cluster and a place for New Yorkers. So the BID team quickly followed up with ambitious, leading-edge programming, including Times Square Arts – a public art programme that provides a platform for innovative contemporary performance and visual arts. Times Square gets 312,000 visitors every day, so it is one of the highest-profile public arts programmes in the world. Supported by an independent advisory group, it has featured diverse works in different media, with the unique backdrop of Times Square the setting for hundreds of prominent and emerging artists.

The speed and scale of this high-profile scheme sent an important signal across the city. Yet many of the most life-enhancing changes happened quietly throughout the city, with space given to smaller-scale pedestrian plazas, road closures, street seats and support – both financial and regulatory – for a roll-out of waterfront parks.

I have been watching the blossoming of one of the largest of these, Brooklyn Bridge Park, ever since it broke ground in 2008. Designed by Michael Van Valkenburgh Associates, this 1.3-mile long, 85-acre riparian public park was created along the East River from the Port Authority's defunct cargo shipping and storage complex. The announcement in 1983 of the authority's intention to sell the complex sparked a debate about how the site could be put to better use as a space for the community, out of which emerged the idea of a park for reconnecting people with the waterfront.

After years of community activism and an intensive planning process, this vision started to become a reality in 2002, when it received a funding commitment from the city and state. This also locked in a provision for the park to become fully self-sufficient when operational.

The industrial waterfront has been shaped from a brownfield site and redundant shipping piers into an urban oasis – a natural landscape of rolling hills and lush gardens encircled by riverfront promenades that offer spectacular city views and a chance to enjoy the waterfront. This is matched equally by the acres of space dedicated to recreation and

Sandbags in Times Square as Hurricane Sandy hit the area on 29 October 2012. Photo: Getty

A New York taxi is stranded in deep water on Manhattan's West Side as Tropical Storm Irene passes through the city. Photo: Rex Features

Times Square gets 312,000 visitors every day, so it is one of the highest-profile public arts programmes in the world

Times Square Arts provides a platform for innovative contemporary performance and visual arts

Industry City is now home to 500 companies. Here, a milliner participates in its community programme

The park offers facilities, including playing fields, a roller rink, barbecue pits and boat launches. Photo: Getty

fun, with a variety of activities and attractions including playing fields, sport courts, playgrounds, barbecue pits, a roller rink and boat launches. Beaches give direct access to the river, making the area the perfect launch pad for kayaking.

Part of its beauty is this diversity of spaces and uses – and, consequently, its users. It is one of the most democratic planned spaces I have experienced and one of my favourite places anywhere, ever. It is not just a wonderful place for people-watching, it is a great spot for listening – a gentle strum of an acoustic guitar, the laughter from a birthday party, the swooshing and squeaking from Pier 2's basketball courts.

Material recycled from its former self is used throughout the park and it has been designed to help recreate the diverse plants, birds and marine life that would have thrived before the area became a hub of industry. Once again home to distinct ecosystems of native woodland, meadows, wetlands and salt marshes, the park is managed with an emphasis on ecology.

The designers carefully considered the shoreline conditions, along with climate change and rising sea levels, to create a park capable of withstanding storms and major floods. Their work was put to the test on 29 October 2012, when Hurricane Sandy battered New York. Sandy's arrival coincided almost exactly with the spring high tide, generating a massive surge of some 14 feet over typical low water. But despite being

More than a third of New Yorkers reported being severely rent burdened and the decline in construction of homes within reach of most wallets and the city's growing population meant the issues at the top of the mayor's in-tray were similar to those facing London mayor Sadiq Khan

submerged in saltwater for hours, the park was able to recover from the inundation relatively speedily.

Sandy killed 43 people and left two million people and 90,000 buildings in the inundation zone without power. It is estimated to have caused $19bn in damage and changed many lives and businesses forever. The impact on transport was tremendous, too, with some 11 million travellers affected.

Bloomberg spent his administration's final year dealing with the significant devastation wrought by the storm – a recovery and rebuilding effort that continues even today.

But the city he handed to his Democratic successor, Bill de Blasio, looked very different from the city he took on. Sandy's impact was felt most acutely in poorer neighbourhoods, adding to an already growing sense of inequality in the city – both New York and London are like catnip to the world's elite, and this 'urban renaissance' brought distinct challenges alongside the positives. More than a third of New Yorkers reported being severely rent burdened and the decline in construction of homes within reach of most wallets and the city's growing population meant the issues at the top of the mayor's in-tray were similar to those facing London mayor Sadiq Khan.

De Blasio entered office in 2014 with an ambitious promise to tackle the city's growing housing problem. He quickly set to work on his housing strategy, 'Housing New York', promising to preserve and create some 200,000 or so affordable housing units (now upped to 300,000).

Housing New York set out a cocktail of measures to achieve this, some highly nuanced and complex, brought forward by the teamwork of the Department of City Planning (DCP) and the Department of Housing Preservation and Development (HPD). Land-use mechanisms and an overhaul of housing programmes and tax incentives were brought together or freshly minted to incentivise and compel developers to meet the new and challenging targets.

The land-use system in New York is based on zoning. 'Inclusionary zoning' is a way to create housing that is affordable for low and moderate income households, by tapping the momentum of the market to develop affordable housing. New York sets out what it wants and what it will provide developers in return, with guidelines and rules tied to a combination of incentives, such as an increase in density or tax abatements.

David Burney, director of urban placemaking and management at the Pratt Institute School of Architecture, served under Bloomberg as commissioner of the Department of Design and Construction. He says: "There are planning cities and deal cities. New York is a deal city."

Part of de Blasio's approach includes a plan to rezone 15 neighbourhoods, allowing for greater density to fit in more homes. Since then, seven of these neighbourhoods have been rezoned, including East New York, Downtown Far Rockaway and East Harlem, and other studies are under way. In these areas, a new 'Mandatory Inclusionary Housing' rule requires developers to provide a percentage of the new homes at 'affordable' rents, with rent levels set by the city.

The foundation of the housing strategy is an inclusive vision of New York's future, committed to protecting residents and

Brooklyn Grange farm covers 5.6 acres of rooftop space

maintaining vibrant, mixed-income neighbourhoods.

Even with this grand aim, an increase in housing is a double-edged sword, since building much-needed homes dramatically alters the character of established, mostly (relatively) low-density neighbourhoods. Lower-income communities are fearful of further gentrification and displacement, so the city has had to work hard to win the acceptance of the multitudes of New Yorkers living in the areas slated for significant growth.

The Office of Neighborhood Strategies was created to help this along. Its task was to truly understand local needs and conditions and deploy a range of tactics, as well as bust the silos that existed across various city agencies. Crucially, it worked to build trust and relationships across the various partners.

One tool created to help with this was the Neighborhood Planning Playbook, which is for communities in rezoned areas to use. Developed in collaboration with relevant city agencies and community organisers, this provides a simple planning process and framework for gathering and sharing information, as well as identifying and solving problems. The desired outcome was to get government and community working together within a shared framework and to make expectations and outcomes clear.

The playbook has brought greater transparency to planning, providing a blueprint for communities to follow. This transparency is mirrored by another city agency, the Department of Small Business Services (SBS), through its neighbourhood services team. A former BID director, deputy commissioner Michael Blaise Backer has a keen eye on what is needed for commercial revitalisation across the city. Focused on the areas in transition, SBS designed its 'Neighborhood 360º' programme to identify,

A Brooklyn Navy yard, a former US Navy shipyard, has leveraged significant private investment to create a modern industrial park that is a centre for modern urban manufacturing and home to 400 businesses, including the largest film and television production studio in the US outside Hollywood

Industry City is home to 500 companies

develop and launch revitalisation projects in partnership with local stakeholders. The result is a comprehensive analysis of the offer and conditions, opportunities and needs, of each commercial district and the populations they serve. SBS's goal is to build capacity for local business and community organisations, so has targeted grants of up to $0.5m to community-based organisations to run each 'commercial district needs assessment'.

SBS hopes this will build resilience within local economies, giving them a much better chance of sustainability, and spread support and opportunity – and therefore equity – for people and businesses beyond established BID areas.

As in London, the city's housing needs have been a dominant issue, with swathes of former industrial land given over to homes and new commercial uses, after traditional industries shrunk. Yet as with London, it is dangerous to let that pendulum swing too far, as we need our cities to function as more than dorms – they are places of employment, services, production and distribution.

New York's officials are busy figuring out how industry can truly co-exist with homes, creating places that are good for people to live in and enjoy while providing space to work and service the metropolis – places that are adaptable for a modern economy.

The shifts in land-use needs are being played out on the city's waterfront, since many industrial buildings are ripe for adaptive re-use, marrying their industrial heritage with new commercial opportunities. There are some enviable examples of this. Brooklyn Navy Yard is a former US Navy shipyard occupying a strategic location on the East River. This 300-acre facility, now owned by New York City, has been transformed by the not-for-profit Brooklyn Navy Yard Development Corporation. Using

the city's funds and land, it has leveraged significant private investment to create a modern industrial park that is a centre for modern urban manufacturing and home to 400 businesses, including Steiner Studios. The studio complex is the largest film and television production studio in the US outside Hollywood, boosting New York's economy by $2.35bn every year.

One of the yard's more unusual tenants is Brooklyn Grange, an organic urban rooftop farm. This is one of three farms situated in Queens and Brooklyn, with 5.6 acres of productive rooftop space dedicated to vegetables and honey that supply local restaurants and markets.

The third and newest farm opened this year just a few miles downstream from Brooklyn Navy Yard. Its growing space graces the rooftop of one of the former factory buildings that now forms Industry City, in Sunset Park, Brooklyn. Originally built as a monumental-scale intermodal manufacturing, warehousing and distribution centre supporting a wide spectrum of businesses, Industry City employed nearly 25,000 workers at its height and was part of Brooklyn's success as a major international seaport. Decline started to set in during the 1960s, and the next 40 years led to a period of disinvestment and decay.

This all changed in 2013 when a new ownership group led by Belvedere Capital and Jamestown began to redevelop Industry City. Its audacious investment programme breathed life into the six million square feet of waterfront space. Covering 35 acres and 16 buildings, Industry City is now home to 500 companies, comfortably straddling the traditional industries that have called it home for decades and the new innovation economy.

Working at such a scale means the 'campus' can have multiple uses, making it a diverse and interesting place to walk around. The Brooklyn Nets basketball team has its headquarters and training facilities here. Not far away, pizza ovens are built and serviced next to milliners, bakers and advanced manufacturers and designers. Already a destination for design and creative events, it is advancing plans to rezone part of its footprint to make provision for two hotels, additional retail space and higher education, making it an even more significant destination.

There are concerns that its growing appeal as a destination and a new, more affluent community bolstered by the rezoning plans will gentrify the traditionally blue-collar neighbourhood. From the outset, CEO Andrew Kimball and his team have been keen to manage that tension, putting the community at the centre of plans – whether that is the occupier strategy, the retail and food offer, or training opportunities. Already, more than a third of the people who work at Industry City live in the surrounding neighbourhoods, and one in every five people lives in or close to Sunset Park.

One of the country's largest adaptive reuse projects in the US, sustainability has always been central to its mission and action. From the outset it has focused on minimising its carbon footprint and has invested $25m in energy infrastructure upgrades. To date, a staggering 14,500 energy-efficient windows have been installed, with the original metal-framed panes deployed throughout the interior. Its approach is also attracting like-minded business – ethically-driven tenants with sustainability and equity at the core of their business models.

Industry City is one of a small number of commercial developers that have signed up to the 'NYC Carbon Challenge'. Aimed at reducing the city's building-based emissions by 30% by 2025, this was originally a Bloomberg initiative, but de Blasio affirmed his commitment to it when he took office. Already, 10 of the pledging companies have met or exceeded the target, putting them in a better place to meet new emissions targets.

Industry City and the Brooklyn Navy Yard are both major players in the city's innovation and tech ecosystem. This has become a fundamental part of its economic growth over the past decade or so, and the city has invested in several dedicated graduate schools centred on technology and urban innovation in the widest sense.

The most significant and highest profile of these is Cornell Tech, an applied science graduate centre born out of a Bloomberg administration international competition. Spotting the need to sustain a skilled talent pool and foster a start-up culture, New York offered $100m and a stretch of city-owned land on Roosevelt Island as the prize. The winning bid – a partnership between Cornell University and Israel's Technion – lost no time in breaking ground and the campus opened in 2017 after several years of operating initial courses out of a Google building in Chelsea.

All the buildings on the campus have been designed to be as energy efficient as possible, with a whole host of features to improve energy use and the quality of the experience in the buildings. They also make enough electricity to be self-sufficient. The campus' main academic centre has nearly 1,500 solar panels on its roof, while in its basement is a geothermal heating and cooling system. This connects to 80 wells drilled 400 feet beneath the site, while a 40,000-gallon underground tank collects rainwater for plumbing, cooling and irrigation systems.

This highly sustainable approach extends to the living quarters for the students and academic staff who have the chance to live on campus in The House. Promoted as the world's first high rise 'passive house', this 26-storey residential tower was designed by the Hudson Companies and Related Companies to consume 60% to 80% less energy than a traditional high rise, for a projected annual saving of 882 tons of CO_2.

Fittingly for a building that houses data and tech scientists, The House provides a steady stream of data for researchers and engineers at work on the campus that in turn feeds further research into energy-saving technologies.

This rather desirable and highly sustainable residence is just one of 73 passive houses being built across New York. These range from brownstones to a 74-storey residential block, and include affordable, multi-family homes being taken forward by the HPD. The first of these was Knickerbocker Commons, a 24-unit, six-storey apartment complex, while Chestnut Commons in East New York, due for completion next year, has 274 homes for very low to low-income families, along with a college and a range of community facilities.

Passive house is just one of HPD's investments in energy-efficient and sustainable affordable housing across New York. To add speed to the mix, HPD is turning to modern methods of construction. Following a call for real estate partners, it has several modular housing developments in train.

One selected developer, Thorobird Companies, is now working in East New York with a local non-profit to build 167 homes for low-income New Yorkers. These homes will

In 2016, the administration released its New York City's Roadmap to 80×50. On 2 June 2017, just one day after President Trump pulled the US out of the Paris climate change agreement, de Blasio signed Executive Order 26, committing New York to the Paris principles. In July this year, New York City Council declared a climate emergency

also benefit from being constructed from modular units manufactured locally by Brooklyn-based FullStack Modular.

HPD's programmes tie into other agencies' work to achieve climate change and resilience goals. A focus on resiliency is fundamental, given the area's increasing vulnerability to rising sea levels and vehement storms. It is not just people living on the waterfront who are vulnerable – neighbourhoods across the city are suffering from the double whammy of climate change and ageing infrastructure, as more frequent and intense heatwaves and downpours bring power failures and extensive flooding.

During Sandy, as the storm water extended way beyond recognised flood zones, buildings that allowed water to flow both in and out survived the inundation with minimal damage. These have pointed the way for a range of policies and approaches to retrofitting and designing for greater resilience.

For DCP, this has meant revising zoning rules, including the emergency regulations put in place following Sandy. Combined with changes to the building codes and land use, this encourages flood-resilient design and construction of coastal property, as well as adaptation of existing properties.

For homeowners in flood-prone neighbourhoods, this means ensuring all habitable space is above a 'design flood elevation', with lower levels used only for storage or parking. DCP's new rules permit changes to the 'zoning envelope' so building owners can build higher to make up for any loss of living space. Elsewhere, thousands of homes are being elevated or constructed on concrete piers.

Resilient neighbourhoods are more than homes that withstand flooding – they are responsive to local needs and conditions. DCP's place-based approach to this adaptation is therefore crucial. As with so much in New York, many communities step forward to be active partners, often taking the lead.

One source of help in stepping up to the challenge are the Waterfront Edge Design Guidelines, which were created to educate and support myriad public and professionals stakeholders about how to "create resilient, ecological, and accessible waterfronts". Masterminded by the Waterfront Alliance, these help coastal communities better respond to the numerous challenges of shaping resilient waterfronts, from sustainable design through to legal structures and access. They offer guidance and case studies, a detailed design guide and an accreditation system that extends beyond New York.

Nevertheless, some still worry that New

Cornell Tech campus was the result of an international competition for $100m and a stretch of land on Roosevelt Island. Photo: Getty

York is not nearly sufficiently prepared for the next Sandy. Indeed, some of my colleagues are cynical about de Blasio's approach to sustainability, thinking it lacks the focus and clarity his predecessor brought to the issue. Some critics point to his lack of leadership on the planned congestion charge.

However, I certainly found a dizzying array of initiatives and policies, strategies and city agencies that are part of the administration's efforts toward sustainability, carbon reduction and resilience. And while Bloomberg made sustainability a central goal of his time in office, de Blasio has looked at the issues through a different lens, weaving growth, sustainability, resilience and equity together in his OneNYC strategy.

What cannot be challenged is that New York's approach to the ticking clock of the climate emergency has hardened in recent years: targets have ratcheted up in line with scientific revelations on the extent of our global crisis.

In 2016, the administration released its New York City's Roadmap to 80×50. This articulated strategies to cut greenhouse gas emissions by 40% by 2030 and 80% by 2050. On 2 June 2017, just one day after President Trump pulled the US out of the Paris climate change agreement, de Blasio signed Executive Order 26, committing New York to the Paris principles.

In July this year, New York City Council declared a climate emergency. This came after passing legislation that will force thousands of medium-sized and large buildings to sharply reduce their greenhouse gas emissions, part of a wider package of bills known as the 'Climate Mobilization Act'. With buildings estimated to account for 67% of emissions, the legislation is a reaction to the failure of the past decade's efforts to achieve voluntary action.

Like London, much of New York's recent real estate is built to high standards of sustainability, while many property owners have retrofitted existing buildings to meet the changing needs and demands of occupiers, as well as energy efficiency.

The legislation is targeted at buildings exceeding 25,000 square feet requiring reductions of 40% in greenhouse gas emissions by 2030 and 80% by 2050. Each building will have an emissions limit based on the property's occupancy group; those that exceed their limits will meet stringent fines.

Critics say the legislation is unfairly designed, placing greater burdens on different occupiers, and is especially punitive to high-occupancy buildings or sectors that have higher energy consumption. Putting in place the measures needed to meet the cap will cost an estimated $4bn, and some building owners are privately saying it will be cheaper to pay the swingeing fines.

To deter this, 2030 penalties are set at $268 per metric ton of CO_2 emitted over the caps, a price point so punitive it will compel building owners to retrofit. Nevertheless, since 50% of buildings are exempt, others say it will not have its intended impact.

The Climate Mobilization Act will keep New York in line with emissions reduction targets set by the Paris agreement. It is heralded by the city's lawmakers as "the single largest carbon reduction effort in any city, anywhere" – the equivalent of taking more than one million cars off the road by 2030.

It also paves the way for a 'Green New Deal', with upwards of a quarter of a million new jobs, some for the likes of the people living in The House, many in construction and maintenance. The goal is to get New York future-fit – to make it a sustainable city that is a great place to live for everyone. The ambition is stretching, the challenges are many and significant.

Remember, though: New York is a deal city.

Patricia Brown is director of consultancy Central. She was CEO of Central London Partnership from 1997-2008, and is contributing editor of The Developer

ULEZ is working, cutting emissions in London significantly

Nicole Badstuber reports on the Ultra Low Emission Zone, an initiative that other cities can emulate to improve their air and shift journeys to public transport

London's air quality is poor – and dangerous. The city is in breach of the EU's legal limits for pollution and levels of particulate matter are greater than the World Health Organization's recommendations.

Poor air quality is detrimental to public health and people's quality of life. It also disproportionately affects vulnerable societal groups, such as children, older people and those suffering from chronic respiratory conditions.

One of the main things London needs to do to improve its air quality and meet its obligations is to reduce its levels of nitrogen oxides (NOx) by 45%. Roughly half of all NOx emissions come from road transport.

A Low Emission Zone (LEZ) covering most of Greater London has been in place since 2008. This applies to lorries and buses all day, every day, with those entering the zone having to meet appropriate emissions standards or pay a daily charge: £100 for larger vans, minibuses and other specialist vehicles, £200 for lorries, coaches and other heavier vehicles.

But in February 2017, mayor of London Sadiq Khan signalled his intention to tackle road transport emissions to a far greater extent. He announced a £10 emissions-based 'toxicity charge' (T-Charge). This came into effect on 23 October 2017 and applied to old, polluting vehicles – broadly, diesel and petrol vehicles registered before 2006 – entering central London. It operated on top of and during the same hours as the £11.50 congestion charge, which operates weekdays from 7am to 6pm.

This marked the start of new political momentum to address air quality in the capital. The T-Charge was seen as the start of an accelerated change in the vehicle fleet, as residents and businesses prepared for the charge.

In April 2017, Khan launched a consultation on a potential replacement for the T-Charge to further tackle the capital's poor air quality – the world's first Ultra Low Emission Zone (ULEZ). Launched on 8 April 2019, ULEZ is one of the cornerstones of the mayor's Air Quality Strategy. It replaced the T-Charge and although it covers the same area as the congestion charge, it operates all day, every day. All vehicles driving in central London must meet tight exhaust standards or pay a daily charge – £12.50 for cars, vans and motorbikes, £100 for lorries and coaches – as well as the congestion charge, to drive in the zone. Buses operating in central London all meet emissions standards so are exempt, as are taxis and registered wheelchair-accessible private hire vehicles.

To accurately review the impact of both the T-Charge and ULEZ, we need to compare figures from before the announcement of the T-Charge in February 2017 with afterwards – although the T-Charge did not take effect until October 2017, the announcement of the charge would have had an effect on individuals' and businesses' choices of vehicles in the intervening period.

Comparing the proportion of compliant vehicles is the most accurate way to track changes in the vehicle fleet, as the number of unique vehicles entering the central London charging zone has also changed since February 2017.

The figures show that over the course of the two-and-a-half years since the announcement of the T-Charge, London has significantly cleaned up the vehicle fleet on its roads. There has been a nearly two-thirds (64%) reduction in the number of older, more polluting, non-compliant vehicles in central London – the equivalent of 39,300 fewer non-compliant vehicles a day.

The introduction of ULEZ accelerated improvements. Fewer and fewer vehicles have entered the central London charging zone since its introduction, the numbers having continued to fall steadily each month since April. On average, 75% of vehicles entering central London now meet the required exhaust standards – nearly double the pre T-Charge level of 39% and more than five percentage points higher than the 69% forecast for ULEZ.

Similarly, 71% of vehicles in April during the 'work week' complied with emission limits – a jump of 10 percentage points from 61% in March. A quarter (9,400) fewer old, polluting, non-compliant vehicles entered the charging zone in April compared to March.

Vehicle numbers have continued to fall since then: in July, there were 35% (12,500) fewer non-compliant vehicles than there were in March.

Not only has ULEZ discouraged driving into central London in polluting vehicles, it has also encouraged the use of public transport. Ticket sales and passenger

Fewer vehicles have entered central London since the introduction of ULEZ, the numbers having continued to fall steadily each month since April. On average, 75% of vehicles entering central London now meet the required exhaust standards

London's Ultra Low Emission Zone, introduced in April 2019, covers the same areas as the congestion charge area but runs all day. Photo: Getty

income are up, particularly on buses and the Underground, with Transport for London (TfL) revising its passenger income forecast for 2019/20 upwards by £29m.

As for the ultimate aim of reducing air pollution from road transport, London air monitoring maps show a shift from moderate to high pollution readings in March to low in April. TfL is expected to publish "impressive" results about the impact of ULEZ on the reduction of NO₂ levels.

An unexpected side-effect of these higher than expected compliance rates is the hit to TfL's bottom line, which potentially adds to its funding worries. Instead of the £77m of revenue from ULEZ originally forecast, TfL is now expecting to take in only £55m – a drop of £22m. By comparison, net income from London's congestion charge in the latest financial year was £147m – £230m income less £83m in tolling, enforcement and administrative costs. Fortunately, the increase in passenger income more than offsets this loss.

These promising results offer other cities a guide to fairly swiftly making their vehicle fleet greener. They indicate travel behaviour responds to pricing mechanisms and while the higher than expected vehicle compliance could worsen TfL's money worries, increased income from buses and the Underground is a promising sign that many are opting for public transport instead of the car.

But London's Air Quality Strategy doesn't stop with ULEZ – the zone will expand in October 2021, bringing in further changes. The bigger zone, 'ULEX', which is also a key part of the UK government's plan to comply with air pollution limits by 2025 or sooner, will cover everywhere between the North and South Circulars – an area encompassing 3.8 million residents. It is expected to reduce NOx pollution by 28% (4,400 tonnes) by 2025.

ULEZ piggybacks on the congestion charge's existing infrastructure and charging processes. Automatic number plate recognition cameras installed at the entry points to the charging zone record the number plates of all vehicles entering the zone. However, ULEX's wider coverage means it will not be able to rely on the existing infrastructure and processes. The cost of the expansion is therefore expected to be £121m, although estimates earlier this year put the price tag at around £700m. The lion's share of spending, £54m, is due in the next financial year (2020/21).

The larger zone's start date is fairly tightly fixed on October 2021, and to change the date or the scope of the expansion materially, a public and stakeholder consultation would have to be conducted.

TfL is also exploring potential options for integrating it into more sophisticated road-pricing systems, which might include pricing based on congestion, emissions and distance, rather than the binary pricing model currently in place.

Another important future development stems from the fact that at the moment, drivers of 38% (10,800) of the non-compliant vehicles entering central London every day are exempt from paying any charge.

That is because residents in and next to the emissions zone are exempt from the charge, in part because its relies on the system and processes put in place for the congestion charge, from which they are also exempt. Residents of the zone also enjoy the highest level of public transport access in the city. Shutting down this exemption could therefore further shift travel behaviour to sustainable modes of transport and free up precious public space used for parking.

Residents' exemption from the charge will expire with the introduction of ULEX, which will also generate greater volumes of data about vehicles entering the wider zone – four times as much as ULEZ. Watch this space for how the end of the exemption might kick-start further shifts in travel behaviour.

Nicole Badstuber is an urban infrastructure researcher at the Centre for Digital Built Britain and University of Cambridge

Many of the adverse outcomes caused by climate change will be psychological, with deleterious impact on mental health and well-being

This summer, London faced its hottest day on record. However, the Greater London Authority did not call a state of emergency – a clear indication that the city was not prepared for or savvy about climate action.

This led to traffic being the same as usual, exposing people to acute levels of air pollution. On the Underground, people were exposed to dangerous levels of heat. In neighbourhoods with vast concrete coverage, vulnerable residents were exposed to high levels of heat stress without respite, increasing the risk of heat stroke and respiratory problems. Furthermore, trains had to be suspended as the tracks became too hot to run a normal service. A summer heatwave 'death spike' was seen in the UK, with deaths per day rising from 1,100 to nearly 1,500, the Office for National Statistics repeated.

In Chicago this January, an extreme winter storm caused by global warming nearly caused the city to grind to a halt. The severe cold weather stopped trains, blew water and gas pipes, and blocked roads. In many instances, these infrastructure weaknesses led to businesses shutting down. The storm also showed how poorly insulated properties are, with many people posting photographs of ice inside their homes.

This all adds up to one thing – cities are not prepared for climate change. This will result in huge costs from loss of life, infrastructure and workforce output as cities grind to a halt. In the US, the costs of not adapting to climate change will be staggering, with heat-related deaths alone set to cost $141bn per year.

Meanwhile, in Europe, southern countries' labour productivity could fall 10-15%. Rising sea levels could result in a fivefold increase in coastal flood damage, affecting more than two million people and wreaking economic tolls of €60bn a year. As extremes of rainfall increase, swollen rivers could expose three times as many people to inland flooding, and the damage from river floods could rise from €5.3m a year to €17.5m.

Most cities already suffer from social inequality. People who are living in poverty,

The vulnerable and poor are going to be affected the most by global warming, this excerpt from the Centric Labs' report, led by Araceli Camargo, shows. But there are measures cities, developers, architects and builders can take

marginalised and discriminated against are suffering the greatest consequences of climate change. This is despite consuming far less than the wealthy, and therefore making a smaller contribution to the problem – poor people commute more by public transport or walk, travel less, use less household energy and consume fewer vanity goods.

Indigenous peoples not only consume far less, they are also at the forefront of climate activism and climate justice. The indigenous people of the Amazon have kept their region safe from deforestation and pollution for decades, and the peoples of Greenland, Canada, the US and the Philippines have addressed similar issues.

The increasing threat of climate change-based disasters will put even more strain on impoverished communities and neighbourhoods. In turn, this will create even greater social inequality in most cities.

The UN says there are three channels through which the inequality-aggravating effects of climate change materialise. The first is the greater exposure of disadvantaged groups to the adverse effects of climate change. It gives the example of recent research that shows tiny particles of air pollution in non-white and low-income communities contain more hazardous ingredients than those in affluent white communities. Communities of colour and those with low education and high poverty and unemployment therefore face greater health risks, even if their air quality meets legal health standards.

The second channel is the increase in the susceptibility to damage caused by climate change. Deprived urban populations tend to live in the most vulnerable locations, usually in infrastructure made from materials that are not resistant to climate change or contingently prepared.

These areas are more susceptible to flooding, storm surges and other extreme weather events such as heatwaves, blizzards, droughts and extreme icing.

Meanwhile, urban expansion in Latin America has resulted in low-income groups occupying areas that are at a higher risk of flooding, seasonal storms and other weather-related catastrophes.

Lastly, there is a decrease in the ability to cope and recover from the damage suffered. Climate change can lead to displacement and homelessness, which in turn makes people even more vulnerable and at risk from its psychological impacts. The loss of home and community, as well as the experience of natural disasters themselves, leaves people unable to cope mentally with future trauma.

In 2005, Hurricane Katrina caused profound devastation to the citizens of New Orleans, especially African-Americans and poor whites. The survivors experienced an "extraordinary array" of known risk factors for heightened pathology, including threat to life, bereavement, exposure to the dead and dying, and lingering social and community disruption.

In 2008, researchers interviewed 810 people and looked at a wide range of trauma pathways: direct experience of physical trauma; seeing physical trauma or death; financial devastation due to loss of home or job, or recovery from injury; experiencing a loss of community; and periods of homelessness or inadequate housing. They found a 16% prevalence of post-traumatic stress disorder (PTSD) among those they interviewed. One of their most interesting findings was that it was the ongoing stressors that contributed to this prevalence.

Homelessness offers no buffer against climate change disasters or day-to-day changes in weather. Research involving 163 homeless services in Australia and New Zealand, for example, found almost one-third of people who have been homeless have suffered extra trauma because of extreme weather.

Similarly, the National Coalition for the Homeless says 700 homeless people die of hypothermia every winter in the US. This number will rise as winter storms become more severe and sustained, as during the January freeze this year.

Homeless people are not only economically vulnerable, they are also mentally and physically more at risk. They suffer from high rates of poorly controlled chronic disease, respiratory conditions and mental illness. These elements add another layer to their climate change vulnerability.

For example, homeless people can become severely sick or die during heatwaves, which are worse in cities because of the urban heat island effect. This in part is because they have existing health problems such as heart disease, which can become more severe because of the

The homeless are hit harder by climate change than the rich. Photo: Alamy

stress of severe heat, especially if they don't receive proper hydration or respite. Cities therefore need specialised severe weather strategies for the homeless, as they will experience the consequences more acutely.

Many of the adverse outcomes caused by climate change will be psychological, with its deleterious impact on mental health and well-being particularly evident in vulnerable populations and ecologically sensitive areas.

The effects on our mental health can be categorised as indirect and direct. Indirect effects can come from the secondary aspects of climate change, such as severe heat or cold. For instance, weather extremes can lead children to stay indoors. Long periods of sedentary behaviour can lead to higher weight, diabetes, anxiety and depression.

There is strong scientific evidence showing how constant stress depletes people's mental health. We can assume that those most vulnerable to climate change will have chronic stress trajectories similar to those living under the chronic stress of impoverished environments.

For example, the indigenous peoples of Greenland, Northern Canada and Alaska are facing a multitude of stressors from the degradation of their habitat at rates similar to those living in impoverished urban environments. They are losing food sources and they are losing family members to accidents in the Arctic's melting ice, despite thousands of years of expertise in reading snow and ice patterns. They are also losing their community to displacement, which can cause deep distress and contribute to the onset of PTSD. Finally, they are experiencing discrimination and marginalisation as governments are not listening to their plights.

All these scenarios add up to a transition into poverty, which will lead to mental health consequences similar to those we have already detailed. Furthermore, those experiencing climate disasters first-hand will

Those developing and managing real estate also have a part to play. Importantly, they must assess buildings and portfolios against climate stresses to note their impact on building sustainability and resilience, as well as human well-being

experience acute trauma, leading some to develop PTSD.

It is of utmost importance for governments to take quick action to shelter people not only from the indirect effects of climate change but from secondary trauma caused by the mishandling of recovery. For example, many who experienced Hurricane Maria, which devastated Dominica, the US Virgin Islands and Puerto Rico in September 2017, are still homeless, adding to their grief and trauma.

For many poor people, climate change is just the beginning of their trauma. Some of those who lived in areas that are no longer inhabitable have tried to migrate to safety. Their journeys and the refugee processes in many countries are causing unimaginable trauma.

Many of the children living in cages in migrant detention centres in the US are there due to climate change. They are showing signs of acute PTSD, with many regressing, losing speech, not recognising their parents, and exhibiting catatonic behaviour.

We risk adding to the global mental health crisis, if we do not respond quickly to the impending dangers caused by climate change.

Not everyone is going to develop PTSD, not even in impoverished communities. However, the rates we have discovered paint a picture of a strained relationship between people and habitats that is only predicted to worsen. Where we live and work should not cause us trauma, should not make us sick, and should not deplete us.

We are living in an era in which we can access a wide range of technologies. We have the capacity to create habits that support us biologically; furthermore, we have the ability to live in a more ecologically friendly way.

Cities should begin implementing more ecological solutions to establish natural ecosystems that will make us more biologically and infrastructurally resilient to climate change.

Best practice and recommendations
Local governments
Local governments should determine the levels of light, noise, urban heat and air pollution their primarily residential communities experience. A good first place to start would be to survey residents to find out what stresses them throughout a given day.

They must also create clearly signed and more efficient intersections and roundabouts to reduce air pollution. Heavily vegetated green spaces in highly urbanised areas will reduce urban heat island effects. Pedestrianising areas will reduce air, noise

Not everyone is going to develop PTSD, not even in impoverished communities. However, the rates we have discovered paint a picture of a strained relationship between people and habitats that is only predicted to worsen. Where we live should not cause us trauma, should not make us sick, and should not deplete us

and light pollution. Warmer street lighting with a smaller radius of luminance will reduce light pollution, as will turning off lights in office buildings at night. Ensuring schools and social and elderly housing are away from main roads will reduce their exposure to air pollution.

New construction practices should be adopted. Construction offers many benefits, such as new infrastructure and services, but it is disruptive to daily lives. Closing roads and pavements to parents with children presents immediate stressors that can result in rerouting through pollution to areas of equally higher pollution. Where this is likely, the stressor impact should be mitigated – for example, by providing clear navigation aids showing how to access blocked amenities.

Cutting and digging also increase emissions of carbon and particulate matter. This can be mitigated by restricting cutting to tents, for example. Similarly, acoustic tents can stop noise pollution affecting those most in need of calm.

Local governments could also consider using smart lighting systems in the public realm. Normally, their output is 20% of their full capacity. However, radar units mounted on lampposts detect pedestrians or vehicles and determine their speed, increasing the lights in their path to full brightness.

Goods deliveries are another area that local governments can address. There are various examples of best practice here, such as implementations by the City of London Corporation (CoLC) and the Grosvenor Estate (GE). CoLC has set standards for large buildings and new developments, which now need to have offsite delivery logistics, while GE has reduced vehicle usage, thus lowering emissions.

This kind of co-ordination of centralised

156

delivery points and non-motorised solutions to last-metre delivery can reduce public realm stress points.

Real estate development and management

Those developing and managing real estate also have a part to play. Importantly, they must assess buildings and portfolios against climate stresses to note their impact on building sustainability and resilience, as well as human well-being.

Extreme weather can decrease the walkability of an area. New housing developments must mitigate unpredictable intense rainfall and wind, which greatly affects elderly citizens' exercising and performing social routines integral to their health. Existing buildings should be adapted or new buildings should be planned to have greater control of the outdoors.

Offices and residential and leisure buildings must afford outside shelter against the wind, rain, and heat. Otherwise, people will be forced further away from the buildings or inside, increasing sedentary behaviour and stress.

Placemaking strategies to induce behavioural change can come through adding opportunities such as EkoFarmer to developments. Encouraging vertical farming in larger developments reduces transport costs for food production. Aerofarms' aeroponic system is a closed loop system that takes the exact same seed from the field and grows it in half the time a traditional field farmer takes. It also uses 95% less water than field farming and 40% less than hydroponics, and is 390 times more productive per square foot than a commercial field farm.

Construction, architecture and engineering

Builders, architects and engineers must adopt new techniques and processes. They must audit supply chains for embodied carbon and ecological stressors. Materiality is often the easiest element to change in construction planning, often offering a mitigation technique when spatial elements cannot be changed.

London-based architect Waugh Thistleton has been leading the commercial application of cross-laminated timber. Products and materials such as this have a three-way benefit: the timber-to-concrete ratio is comparatively lower for the same construction; fewer vehicles are therefore involved in transporting it through neighbourhoods; and it is a natural product, so more ecologically responsive and adaptable to climate change – nature has been in R&D for 4.5 billion years.

However, new, artificial materials are also

The Coast Guard assesses damage in New Orleans, following Hurricane Katrina. Photo: Getty

available. CarbonCure has a technology that adds recycled CO_2 to fresh concrete. 'CO_2 mineralisation' converts CO_2 to a mineral and so becomes permanently captured, rather than emitted into the atmosphere. Better still, this process makes concrete better. So far, 63.6 million pounds of CO_2 have been mineralised – the equivalent of 34,619 acres of forestland absorbing CO_2 for a year.

Another firm, Solidia Technologies has patented processes that ease production, reduce costs, and improve the performance of cement and concrete, while reducing the carbon footprint of concrete up to 70% and water use up to 100% during manufacturing.

Those involved in construction should also review existing building guidelines.

Sustainable Homes on behalf of the London Climate Change Partnership produced a report in January 2013 that identified a series of post-occupancy evaluations that can be used to prepare social homes for climate change. These principally covered water efficiency, overheating, and flood risk. The cost of adaptation was £2.7m over and above the Decent Homes requirements. However, residents were projected to save £75,000 per year through lower heating costs and reductions in water use.

Find out more

Read the full report at www.thecentriclab.com/ptsd-cities

Who benefits from private sector placemaking?

Despite the successes of the past decades, there are definite losers from privately owned public spaces, the Van Alen Institute's International Council discovers. Christine Murray reports

The Bedford Estate, one of London's 16 great estates, is a touchstone for British architects, with its handsome, Georgian terraced houses and garden squares. The fact that the estate also contains the country's most famous architecture school, the AA, which counts Zaha Hadid and Richard Rogers among its alumni, elevates its status to mythic.

But the palpable reaction of members of the Van Alen Institute's International Council is not of delight. The 19-strong group of architects, engineers and urban designers are with me on a field trip to the estate, which is owned by the Russell family. Standing in the family's private grounds, surrounded by the backs of terraced houses, the group is full of questions.

"You mean the people living in these houses can't use this garden?" asks one architect, staring at the back doors of the homes, which open onto a black, wrought-iron fence.

"No, but the hotel that backs onto this garden can host weddings here," explains Simon Elmer, steward of the Bedford Estate.

"Host weddings... in the residents' garden?"

"It's not the residents' garden."

It is an apt start to 'Private means to public ends: the role of the private sector in city making' – a tour of the capital's privately owned public spaces (POPS) and the idiosyncratic rules and inherent compromises that characterise them.

Stacey Anderson, associate director of business development and special initiatives at Van Alen, says the topic was inspired by the contentious opening of Hudson Yards in Manhattan. The US$25bn New York development sparked outcry over its use of US$5.6bn in taxpayer subsidies, as well as its policy, since rescinded, that personal photographs taken of its centrepiece structure, Vessel, were owned by Hudson Yards' developer Related.

The New York-based Van Alen Institute arranges twice-yearly trips such as these, as part of the 125-year-old, not-for-profit's mission to "catalyse positive change in cities".

International Council, with Building Centre's model of London. Photo: Marina Piedade

Its International Council, founded in 2014 with Kai-Uwe Bergmann of the Bjarke Ingels Group, aims to "expand Van Alen's mission to improve cities globally", bringing together thought leaders from around the world to investigate urban issues.

The current chairs are Alfredo Caraballo and Daniel Elsea of Allies and Morrison, and Carl Backstrand and Monica von Schmalensee of White Arkitekter.

London's relationship to POPS is long and deep-rooted. The great estates are part of the city's psyche and are seen as benevolent contributions. According to Dr Patrice Derrington, director of the real estate development programme at Columbia University, the Bedford Estate is the oldest example in the world of private, speculative real estate, beginning with the land deal in Covent Garden.

Over three days, the tour puzzles over the benefits and trade-offs of the free market designing the marketplace. My role, as embedded journalist, is to take the pulse of the attendees and ask difficult questions. It also falls to me and other London-based attendees to provide context.

If love and football are shared international languages, bureaucracy is not. The peculiarities of the planning system, Community Infrastructure Levy and Section 106 contributions, leaseholds versus freeholds, affordable rent (and how it is not really affordable), shared ownership, the role of housing associations, council housing and the Right to Buy make explaining the offside rule sound like child's play.

On a guided tour through central Somers Town in north-west London, we hear how the public sector is forced to make compromises, too, in order to self-fund the construction of facilities in an age of cuts. Here, on 2.2 hectares of the London Borough of Camden's land, the sale of new housing funds affordable housing, community facilities and a new public park, on land freed up by squeezing the playgrounds of a school.

Deborah Saunt, partner at architecture studio DSDHA, which undertook the masterplan, explains that the grounds were reduced and a play court stacked, in order to create a series of linked green spaces and clear land for apartment blocks.

At King's Cross Central, the 67-acre private estate developed by Argent Related where Google, Universal Music and YouTube have their offices, notable is the private security, ground rules and how the development knits into the city. The visitors admire the scale, quality and ambition of the architecture and its vast public spaces, including parks, canal-side steps and Granary Square.

Members of the Van Alen Institute admiring the repurposed former Olympic Park. Photo: Marina Piedade

Unlike Somers Town, which is an ordinary piece of city, the King's Cross campus is cut off from surrounding (deprived) neighbourhoods and patrolled by the red caps, who provide information, cleaning services and security.

They also enforce the site's many arbitrary regulations, which one source says include "anything that might hurt or offend you or someone else". You can ride a skateboard or carry a ball, but you can't do a skateboarding trick or kick a football; you can take photographs, but not with a tripod. None of this is written down, so you are free to do what you like... until you aren't.

Recent revelations about the use of facial recognition technology at King's Cross add to the creepiness – not least because the technology is said to be 95% inaccurate. It is rumoured that high-end department stores in London are investing in the technology, too, to identify big spenders and shoplifters alike: humans are increasingly data points to be pondered over and manipulated into further shopping, drinking or eating.

In contrast, a visit to the Olympic Park – also a private estate with its own CCTV cameras and security – is a feel-good moment. The wide-open green spaces, renewed canals, wild-flower meadows, playgrounds and impressive leisure facilities, including the Aquatics Centre and the velodrome, are seen as genuinely altruistic. Repurposing the curious great shed of Here East into offices, a future museum and a university outpost is forward-thinking, too, in the context of net zero carbon, when you think the other option is demolition.

But if the park is a gift to this neighbourhood, the compromise is found in the new cityscape that edges it. The hodgepodge skyline around Stratford Station is described by the Van Alen visitors as a "mess", the housing of East Village is "strangely suburban" and "seemingly deserted", while the new developments of Hackney Wick and Fish Island are dismissed as "generic".

"I could be anywhere," says one architect.

Vastint's Sugar House Island development is named after the sugar trade, despite its associations with slavery. This seems more than a little inappropriate for a fancy housing development in one of the most deprived boroughs in the country

"I don't know how they're getting away with it."

To the outsider architect, where the new architecture of east London isn't hideous, it is boring. Local architects and developers speak smugly of the designs riffing on the aesthetic of warehouses and sheds. But it is pointless to riff on a neighbourhood of demolished low-rent industrial buildings that were only cool because they once housed the biggest concentration of artists in Europe.

Whether new development or future rendering, whether housing, offices or mixed-use co-working incubator spaces, the so-called 'brown biscuit architecture' of London's planning-friendly vernacular looks as bland and flavourless as a digestive.

Riffing on the past has dangerous connotations, too. Vastint's Sugar House Island development is named after the sugar trade, despite its associations with slavery. This seems more than a little inappropriate for a fancy housing development in one of the most deprived boroughs in the country. The fact that there is no affordable or social housing on the whole island doesn't help either.

Asked whether they had concerns about this becoming a middle-class gated island in a sea of poverty, Vastint UK's regeneration manager Valli van Zijl says the generous public spaces were a gift that would serve and

The King's Cross estate has CCTV cameras and deploys facial recognition technology across the campus. Photo: Getty

attract people from local neighbourhoods.

As to why there is no affordable housing at Sugar House Island, a source close to the project reveals the local council (Newham) said it had enough poor people: "They didn't need any more poor-people housing. They were trying to attract people with money."

The east London developments also share a relaxed attitude to climate change, despite their location near the River Lea and its marshes. Some of the new buildings have been raised up or feature newly reinforced banks along the canal.

But in this high-risk flood zone, uneven

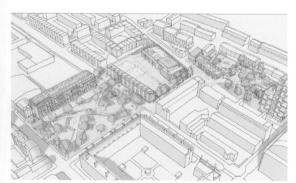

Central Somers Town gains green space at the expense of a school playground

flood protection will make rising waters worse for surrounding communities. Planning documents for Hackney Wick justify construction here because of the pressing need for housing.

But when asked about the inevitability of flooding, architects and developers are blasé, except to say that buildings comply with rules and regulations. There is also unshakeable belief in the Thames Barrier – designed to protect London from a tidal surge until 2030, after which its standard of protection will slowly decline.

As the Van Alen International Council tour comes to an end, it strikes me that there is a certain smugness in the industry about the scale of what has been achieved in London over the past decade. Certainly, the projects do impress. But who benefits? London homelessness hit a record high in 2018 after an 18% rise. In the boroughs we visit – Hackney, Tower Hamlets, Newham, Camden and Islington – roughly 40% of children live in poverty after housing costs. New developments have alienated less-affluent neighbours and dispersed fragile communities: the artists of Hackney Wick have been displaced, the housing estates that surround King's Cross are still impoverished,

and 'Olympic-legacy' borough Newham has the highest rate of homelessness in England.

As for POPS, their idiosyncrasies are the product of a city reluctant to undertake capital projects and instead haggling for a cut of the property boom. On a spreadsheet, this model can look win-win, but for the citizen, there is no such thing as a free lunch: enjoying a concert in the POPS square means ceding your freedom of assembly, protest and privacy. Too many of these new communities have invisible gates.

Before the next phase of negotiation, compromise and construction begins, we need to develop a more sophisticated measure of success than city beautification and open access to public space. Will the residents of these places be better off?

Find out more
www.vanalen.org

HOMES UK
THE FUTURE OF LIVING
27-28 November 2019, ExCeL, London

REGISTER
TO ATTEND

CREATING QUALITY HOMES IN THRIVING COMMUNITIES

- Gain a "big picture" overview and connect with the residential property market

- Access tailored content for each tenure including Build to Rent, student accommodation, retirement living, intergenerational and co-living, affordable housing and more

- Hear fresh ideas to tackle shared challenges

- Understand opportunities for collaboration and expansion

Key agenda topics will cover:

| ASSET MANAGEMENT | RESIDENTIAL DEVELOPMENT | PLACEMAKING | LAND & PLANNING | BUILD TO RENT | MMC |

FOR THE **FULL AGENDA** AND TO **REGISTER TODAY** VISIT
HOMESEVENT.CO.UK 🐦 @HOMESEVENT 🔗 /HOMES-EXHIBITION

Regional champions

Despite its strengths, Coventry and Warwickshire's economic performance was just average. **Adam Dent** reveals how the region learned to tell its own story so it could fulfil its potential

Coventry and Warwickshire is proof that a successful place is more than simply a collection of assets.

The area is one of the most accessible in the UK, set right at the heart of the country's transport network, and has all the attributes an area needs to thrive. It has a major city, wonderful historic towns, fantastic leisure assets, a wonderful natural environment, a very strong industrial and commercial base, and two major award-winning universities.

Yet for many years, it was not the sum of its parts. Economic performance was average – despite the above-average attributes – and it suffered from an image problem. That has changed.

The advent of the Coventry and Warwickshire Local Enterprise Partnership (CWLEP), designed to drive the economy forward, and the birth and subsequent success of the Coventry and Warwickshire Place Board have brought deep-seated changes, the fruits of which are now being realised.

The Place Board was formed in 2012 and Les Ratcliffe, a former senior executive at Jaguar Land Rover, has chaired the board from day one. He believes a combination of factors – backed by a co-ordinated effort – have really propelled the area to a new level.

He says: "I think, like many areas, people were trying to do good things to improve Coventry and Warwickshire, but there was no sense of shared purpose or common goals. That has now changed beyond recognition.

"The Place Board was really the brainchild of Martin Reeves, the chief executive of Coventry City Council, who realised that some focus was badly needed to fulfil our potential as a place to live, work, play and invest in.

"He commissioned 'Thinking Place' to really look at Coventry and Warwickshire and draw up the story of it as a place. A board, made up predominantly of interested and driven private sector members, was brought together to build upon that work."

One of the main initiatives was to create a 'champions' scheme that would enable businesses and organisations to tell the story of Coventry and Warwickshire.

Six years after its formation, the champions scheme is now a very strong network, with bi-monthly meetings that regularly attract an audience of 200.

Ratcliffe adds: "The power of our champions scheme has been one of the main successes. We attract speakers who have a strong connection with our area but are, more often than not, operating at a national level.

"They have to bring something fresh to our meetings, because informing the audience is vital, not only to attracting them but also – more importantly – to getting them to act as our network, spreading word of everything happening here.

"We have unearthed key figures who live or work in this area who we never would have known about. They range from a woman originally from this area whose company won a special effects Oscar, through the CEO of one of the largest dining chains in the UK, to the designer of the first all-electric superbike.

"None of them had been heard in this area; all had fascinating stories – stories rooted here."

The sense that Coventry and Warwickshire had not used its assets to attract and host major events was also manifested through the scheme. When that potential was explained at an early meeting, it struck a chord.

One champion could not believe there was no event to celebrate the fact the city was the centre of the UK motor industry. Stirred on by the challenge laid down, he formed MotoFest, which in a few short years became the premier city-centre event of its type, attracting 140,000 weekend visitors.

Another champion was inspired by Thinking Place's themes of 'events' and 'peace and reconciliation' to found Rising – a global peace and conflict-resolution symposium that brings key figures from across the world.

Those two major events have been joined by others – the OVO Energy Women's

> **"The LEP has ensured that we have to act as one. The private sector does not really recognise civic boundaries and it was important that ethos was shared and the LEP has made it happen"**

Sponsored feature

The National Automotive Innovation Centre at the University of Warwick. Image: Nick Dimbleby

Tour, the OVO Energy Tour of Britain, the Big Weekend – which have brought major attractions to the area for local people and visitors. The 2022 Commonwealth Games will bring judo, wrestling, rugby sevens and lawn bowls to Coventry and Warwickshire.

The Place Board now sits under the auspices of the CWLEP, which Ratcliffe believes has been instrumental in improving Coventry and Warwickshire as a place.

"For many years, the town and county were often politically opposed and there was, to be honest, a level of chippiness and resentment.

"The LEP has ensured that we have to act as one. The private sector does not really recognise civic boundaries and it was important that ethos was shared and the LEP has made it happen."

That was no more in evidence when Coventry won the right to be the 2021 UK City of Culture. It was primarily a bid by the city, but won the full support of the whole area. Warwickshire County Council has leant support and has given its financial backing, while companies from across the area have contributed.

Ratcliffe added: "To see Warwickshire in the heart of Coventry, celebrating on the night we were announced as UK City of Culture, was for me a telling moment. It proved that we had made real progress.

"That unity has created a real sense of place that has allowed us to make huge steps that benefit local people and visitors, which would just not have been possible before.

"A great deal of that work has deliberately gone on below the radar but it has given us the purpose and pride to be more ambitious in what we set out to achieve – and the unity has allowed us to make it happen."

'Godiva Awakes' will play an important part in Coventry's 2021 UK City of Culture events

A festival is not a conference

The Developer's inaugural Festival of Place welcomed 450 participants to consider how to make cities that thrive. It also saw the live judging and awarding – to the sound of a mariachi band – of the first ever The Pineapples awards, writes Christine Murray with photos by John Sturrock

The market square at the heart of the Festival of Place

On 9 July at Tobacco Dock in east London, we launched *The Developer*'s major annual event, the Festival of Place (the next will be on 7 July 2020). This first year, 450 participants attended, including private and public sector developers, local and national government, cities, investors, architects, landscape designers, scientists, academics, charities, community outreach workers, activists, artists, and other makers of place. They came together to consider how to make cities that thrive in the context of large-scale, urban redevelopment in the UK.

In response to feedback from members of the property and architecture market saying they are tired of the same old conferences, this one-day happening is dynamic, with five stages of simultaneous and compelling content: Festival Hall, sponsored by Places for People; Town Hall; Community Centre; and two stages presenting projects shortlisted for The Pineapples awards for place.

The idea of a festival is that everyone is free to move around, watching 15 minutes of one act before going to see another. Participants have the freedom to shape their days, but that means they can leave partway through talks. The emergent culture of the festival has to make that OK.

Equally important is the space between the sessions – the Market Square and High Street, with street furniture provided by Vestre, is designed to encourage spontaneous conversations. The coffee is on tap and lunch that caters for the dietarily diverse is included in the price of the ticket.

The 46 speakers – 48% women and 17% BAME – included: leading developers such as Dan Labbad, chief executive officer, Europe, for Lendlease, and Sir Stuart Lipton, partner at Lipton Rogers Developments; scientists and researchers such as Araceli Camargo from Centric Lab and Chanuki Illushka Seresinhe from The Alan Turing Institute; government figures such as Rachel Fisher, deputy director for regeneration and infrastructure at the Ministry of Housing, Communities and Local Government; city-shapers such as Tim Tompkins, president of the Times Square Alliance; leading designers such as Bob Allies of Allies and Morrison, Dinah Bornat of ZCD Architects, and Cannon Ivers of LDA Design; and a range of culture, community outreach and arts specialists.

Our ambition was to create a safe space for city-shapers and makers to open their minds, share frankly, participate, inspire, celebrate and learn. Participants could attend a walking tour of London Dock, experience the city from 95cm – the average height of a three-year-old – with the Urban95 VR experience, or hang out in the market square and enjoy a selection of stalls from our supporters, including free Monmouth Coffee Company coffee courtesy of Scott Brownrigg, Wembley Park IPA and pilsner from Quintain, and fresh fruit from Savills Urban Design Studio. There was also the chance to adopt a bat, thanks to the Partnership for Biodiversity in Planning, and flowers were available from Elizabeth Marsh Floral Design.

The Placehack workshops are designed to speak creativity. Participants can roll up their sleeves and network while gaining new skills and having fun. Attendees could build small-scale models of cities using salvaged and scrap material with the founder of Kiondo, Andre Reid, reimagine cities for young families with Urban95, explore authenticity and the branding of place with founder of dn&co Joy Nazzari, and experiment with the shape of public spaces to affect behaviour with Professor Nick Tyler, Chadwick chair of civil engineering at UCL.

Design Council, one of the sponsors of this year's festival, working with Jacobs, Mike Saunders, CEO and co-founder of Commonplace, and Charles Campion, partner at JTP Architects, ran a two-hour workshop on creating a greener, liveable, lovable city. Young students and urbanists had the chance to tell us what is most important to them in developing the places and society they would like to live in. Encouraged to share their ideas and visions of a place in which they wanted to live, work and play, their responses were the seeds for a Manifesto for Change (see right).

As for celebration, the live judging of The Pineapples awards for place happened all day, with placemakers from nominated projects presenting their work to the judging panel in front of the audience. The winners were announced at the close of the day at a party, accompanied by a mariachi band, in the Festival of Place pub.

We commissioned a live placetest of the Festival of Place 2019 by anthropologist and social researcher Nitasha Kapoor to tell us about the behaviour and attitude of our participants. Her study of the day revealed the power of carving out a 'liminal space' in shaping an industry conversation, and the important role of chairs and communicators. Read more on the following pages and see the winners of the inaugural The Pineapples.

And see you next year! Save the date: 7 July 2020.

Festival of Place has been nominated for the award for IBP Event of the Year 2019

Find out more
www.festivalofplace.co.uk

Manifesto for Change
Power to nature, place, people

This manifesto was formed through the Placehack: Greener, Liveable, Loveable at Festival of Place 2019. It is a call to attention created by an international group of the next generation who will inherit the responsibility of designing our spaces and places. This is a conceptual framework for the future of place.

1. Let nature in
Use nature-based solutions and systems as a driver of design, where nature can be embedded into our everyday landscapes. Cities will become 'bio havens', designed for pollinators, designed for biodiversity, designed for humans to connect with nature. We will rewild the city. Buildings, streets and parks will become working landscapes, through agroforestry, food growth and farming, on a city-wide scale. Landscape design and natural systems will be a must-have and not a nice-to-have.

2. Walking and cycling rules
We will prioritise pedestrians, cyclists and public transport. We will reduce car-use and work towards alternatives to private and freight vehicles. Travel will be active, with the freedom to move in and engage with our surroundings. Inclusivity will be at the core of all transport schemes.

3. Shape and own our places
Engagement in design will be meaningful. Politicians and design professionals serve the community and not their own agendas. Total collaboration at the earliest stage will create a drive for ownership. Engagement with everyone, every time. We will seek out school and youth groups, resident groups, and engage from commission to completion and following handover.

4. Embrace the spirit of experimentation
Public spaces will be flexible for experimentation through temporary installations, markets, festivals and displays. We will challenge the design of publicly accessible spaces to be inclusive and create interaction and opportunities to play for every user.

5. Eradicate loneliness, eradicate isolation
We will create spaces for people to meet, collaborate and connect with each other, across generations and cultures. Housing should create opportunities to bring people together, explore, create and experiment. We feel that access to healthy and inclusive environments is a basic human right.

The festival was a safe space for city-shapers and makers to open their minds, share frankly, participate, inspire, celebrate and learn

Dr Patrice Derrington gave a keynote speech in which she talked about a development industry that is fragmented – and always has been

Who are these people "who care about making places that thrive"?

Anthropologist Nitasha Kapoor went into the field to learn what kind of visitors the Festival of Place attracted this year and how they interacted on the day. Why have they decided it is worth their while to take a day out of work to be here? And how might this type of gathering help solve these problems?

Days before the Festival of Place, the organiser and editor-in-chief of *The Developer* Christine Murray wrote in *Dezeen* that she founded the event "in the hopes that by getting a jumble of smart people and professionals together, we can start to unpick these problems and find a way forward".

The problems she refers to are complex and interconnected: a climate emergency, an epidemic of homelessness, a mental health crisis, and more.

As I arrived at the Festival of Place, charged with undertaking a live 'placetest' of the event, that idea of "a jumble of smart people" stuck with me. Who are these people "who care about making places that thrive", as Murray puts it? As an anthropologist and social researcher, that is what I was there to find out.

The inaugural festival brought together 450 developers, planners, investors, researchers, consultants, architects, community organisers, activists and designers – professionals across multiple disciplines linked by their interest in urban redevelopment.

Why have they decided it is worth their while to take a day out of work to be here? And how might this type of gathering help solve these problems?

As for the venue, it is interesting to consider the place where 'place' is being discussed. Tobacco Dock has always been about money, markets and the progress of capitalism. Beginning with the world trade in tobacco, then a failed shopping centre, it is now a venue for weddings, exhibitions and other corporate and commercial events. The interior design highlights its trade heritage,

with exposed iron girders, wooden beams and bare brick walls. Yet trade has long since given way to PowerPoint, plastic chairs and Post-it notes.

Placetesting does not preclude participation: I listened to presentations about regeneration, crime and the future of work, attended panels on the citizen-as-developer and curating culture, and took part in workshops to reimagine places, considering the health of future generations and the planet. I talked to people I knew and those I didn't, and asked for their thoughts on the day. I kept my eyes and ears open, and took notes.

What I found was that people came to this gathering for different reasons. They were presenting, competing, learning, sharing, socialising, networking or simply having a day away from their desks. The programme was more eclectic than at most architecture and development conferences, an ambition reflected in the fact that this was officially a 'festival' and not a conference – although the rituals and norms associated with attending a conference are strong, so people mostly behaved more in line with a business environment than a field in Glastonbury.

There was a level of joy and fun in the programming that increased the chances of learning something or meeting someone new. Several people told me that they were there to witness and be a part of something that was different from the start.

Whether a conference or a festival, the liminal quality of these work-not-work environments means we are more likely to have a new experience, and that was certainly true at the Festival of Place. Liminality is a concept explored and developed by Victor Turner, a British anthropologist who was especially interested in rituals and rites of passage. The liminal state is one where people are removed from the normal structures of society due to some sort of 'tension' and in so doing they become 'betwixt or between' – neither fully here nor there, and possibly both.

> There was a level of joy and fun in the programming that increased the chances of learning something or meeting someone new. Several people told me that they were there to witness and be a part of something that was different from the start

An example of a classic liminal phase would be the period of time between passing exams or handing in final assignments and the graduation ceremony or first job – the student is no longer studying but has not started the next phase of life and is in a sort of no man's land.

Liminal states are periods of time when people can try out things and be experimental, a 'perhaps' state of mind. Anything might – or even should – happen. Turner called the people who share liminal states the 'communitas'. He explained that this group creates strong bonds and a camaraderie in the attempt to work through whatever tension is being experienced.

People had gathered at the Festival of Place to discuss and tackle those big problems. They wanted to figure out what could possibly heal the crisis and play a part.

Liminality became a theme that I continued to notice throughout the day. Anne Power, emeritus professor of social policy at LSE, spoke of the importance of half-acre infill sites – often the places that develop organically in between other places. She advocated leaving them as they are or enhancing them, rather than filling them in or using them as a reason to start a development from scratch.

Professor Nick Tyler, Chadwick chair of civil engineering at UCL, talked about how "places are people", reminding us that without a deep understanding of people and culture, there is little chance of creating and sustaining strong places.

Prompted by these two speakers in particular, I started noticing and thinking about those who fall between people – the facilitators.

In liminal rituals, there is an understanding that people will not stay in this state for long – a conference is just for one day. Crucially, they are not alone but guided by 'ceremony masters', guides who often mediate between what happens there and what comes next.

At the Festival of Place, I saw 'guides' everywhere. They were the hosts of the day, chairing panels, leading workshops, standing in the wings, introducing and greeting, actively listening, and connecting people and ideas together. They were the shapeshifters who translated presentations into possibilities for creativity.

Guides play a role that is barely noticed until it isn't done well, such as when there isn't enough time left to ask questions of a panel or you are asked by someone who missed a talk what happened and you don't have anything interesting to say. Or when the coffee is bad.

Without these small and thoughtful details, we are left with an experience that

People came to this gathering to present, compete, learn, share, socialise, network or simply have a day away from their desks

Whether a conference or a festival, the liminal quality of these work-not-work environments means we are more likely to have a new experience

is predictable, that doesn't come to life. Without those guides and their skills, we are left with presentations of fact, without the chance to build on it.

I was struck by the ease with which these guides moved in a place filled with people who are unfamiliar to each other. That was most clearly signposted by what attendees chose to wear: suits, business casual, summer dresses, trainers, backpacks, folded Brompton bikes. These choices signal the different types of work happening at the conference, but also reveal different economic and social backgrounds and, likely, different politics and perspectives on places and people.

Dr Patrice Derrington, professor and director of the real estate development programme at Columbia University in New York, gave a keynote speech in which she talked about a development industry that is fragmented – and has always been. Global financial flows have little in common with community-organised events; people who are comfortable working in risk analysis, spreadsheets and bottom lines are generally at a distance from those working with the community, stories and human potential. Yet they are all trying to make places that thrive, connected by the guides who seem to know everyone or want to get to know everyone in the room.

I talked to several of the guides at the conference and recognised a pattern in their stories. They can speak to different types of people and, when necessary, translate those ideas for others.

Emma Warren, author of *Make Some Space*, a book about how to help culture thrive, advocated on stage for the importance of 'relationship managers' – people who understand both sides of the coin and who can mediate between different environments.

Ash Patel, community engagement officer at Quintain's The Yellow, a community hub in Wembley Park, told me about how he and colleagues might run a community workshop in the morning and demonstrate its impact to middle-managers and directors in the afternoon.

Dinah Bornat, founder of ZCD Architects, translates the natural ways in which kids play into the language of masterplanning. Bornat developed innovative mapping techniques off the back of countless hours observing and talking to kids about their daily lives and local neighbourhoods for a better understanding of how children use space and what they need.

How do you recognise a guide? When they were young, they were probably the kids at school who were friends with a few different cliques, moving between them, popular without being front and centre. They took an

Experiencing the city as a three-year-old

Quintain laid on pilsner and IPA

'odd path' to get to where they are; it was not what they set out to be or do, and remains unexpected and surprising. It is obvious in the way they tell stories about their work that they love what they do.

Patricia Brown, director at urban consultancy Central, spoke to me about the importance of hospitality – including food and drink to the extent that she uses it as a defining feature of her manifesto, the often overlooked importance of creating the right vibe in the room to get people comfortable and setting the right conditions for positive conversations.

Over lunch, Warren told me about how her ideal gathering would be to invite people to a place, give them delicious food and drinks, and leave them be, believing that the best conversations often come from a place of generosity and simplicity.

These are people attracted to complex problems and they like trying to solve them. They aren't afraid to acknowledge the scale of the current ones: the word 'crisis' was repeatedly used on and off stage. The numbers are striking: an estimated half of all polluting emissions come from development and construction, in part due to the basic building blocks of concrete, glass and steel. More people in the industry are beginning to

understand that they must be smarter, better and take responsibility for their role in the problem. Or else what?

"It is still not too late to act," said climate activist Greta Thunberg recently. "It will take a far-reaching vision, it will take courage, it will take fierce, fierce determination to act now, to lay the foundations where we may not know all the details about how to shape the ceiling. It will take 'cathedral thinking'."

These guides thrive when faced with knotty problems and they often share that kind of cathedral thinking: they know there is work to be done and they know there must be a way through, even if we don't yet know every step of the way. And, of course, you can't build a cathedral on your own.

During his workshop, Tyler asked the question at the heart of good places: "How do you get people to trust each other?" The people who can stand firmly with one foot in the land of numbers and business, the other in the land of people and stories, can help to galvanise a fragmented industry. They gain the trust of different groups by finding commonalities, rather than dwelling on differences. They are community organisers, urban consultants, business academics. They are the people writing reports, editing magazines, researching and campaigning. They are trusted sources of knowledge and goodwill for the industry because they have specialist knowledge and their motives are to make the industry better. They are the people you call when you have a really difficult problem, something that hasn't been done before, that needs a different approach and a different group of people on the case.

Sometimes it takes a big gathering to see who turns up, who shines bright and whom you can call the next day to make places that thrive. The Festival of Place was ambitious, and it happened. Hundreds of people were there and according to the post-event online survey, two-thirds say they are likely or extremely likely to attend again, with just one person saying they are unlikely to come back.

What I learned during the live placetest was that we have strong and mighty guides among the makers of place, and they play a critical role as informed hosts, gathering different types of people together, making sure everyone feels like they are getting what they need, and challenging us to do better.

Find out more
Next year's Festival of Place will take place on 7 July at Tobacco Dock

The programme was more eclectic than at most business conferences, reflected in the fact it was officially a 'festival'

Winners of The Pineapples awards for place

Showcasing the best in placemaking in the UK

The Pineapples, sponsored by the Design Council, celebrate the urban life of developments and places where people want to live, work and play. The four categories were: Completed Place, Place in Progress, Contribution To Place for individual buildings and meanwhiles, and Future Place for masterplans.

The awards are unique because all shortlisted projects are visited by the judges, as well as presented to a live audience at the Festival of Place. They also require completed projects to be in use for at least two years before they can be assessed, in an attempt to judge the life of the place.

The winners were announced at the close of the Festival of Place in the on-site pub, accompanied by a mariachi band.

The Design Council said: "We are proud to sponsor the Festival of Place and The

Pineapples awards, the summer's leading event in the built environment calendar. Our experience and evidence show that well-designed neighbourhoods can have a transformational impact on us all, improving health and well-being, enhancing the environment, and stimulating the economy."

The judges

Ben Adams, founding director, Ben Adams Architects

Yolande Barnes, chair, Bartlett Real Estate Institute, UCL

Dinah Bornat, co-founder, ZCD Architects

Joe Covill, operations director, This is Projekt

Catherine Dewar, regional director – North West, Historic England

Eleanor Fawcett, head of design, Old Oak and Park Royal Development

Mike Gedye, executive director, CBRE

Emily Gee, regional director, London and South East, Historic England

Brian Ham, executive director – development, Home Group

Akeel Malik, fund manager, Urban Splash Residential Fund

Kate Martin, director of city housing, City of Wolverhampton Council

Peter Martin, group director – development, Sanctuary Group

Sue Morgan, director of architecture and the built environment, Design Council

Martin Reeves, chief executive, Coventry City Council

Piers Taylor, founder, Invisible Studio Architects

Roisin Willmott, director of Wales and Northern Ireland, Royal Town Planning Institute

The Pineapple for Completed Place

Winner: Balham High Road, London – Wandsworth Borough Council, Metropolitan Workshop
Balham has undergone much change, as young professionals and families, priced out of Clapham, moved into the area. The town centre and streetscape was in need of improvement. The scheme to overhaul the public realm included transforming Hildreth Street into a vibrant market square with a cafe strip and finding a creative solution to the 'ugly wall', a flank wall that is now covered in mock-Victorian green faience tiling as a nod to the Northern line. Footfall in the centre of Balham is now up 30% and vacancy rates have fallen.

Judges' comments:
"Balham High Road went beyond the brief, having significant social impact through a creative range of placemaking interventions, a catalyst for local retailers and residents, and excellent engagement and process"

The Pineapple for Future Place

Winner: West End Project, London – London Borough of Camden, LDA Design
The West End Project is a radical overhaul of traffic and public realm in central London. It removes the one-way systems and general traffic on Tottenham Court Road and Gower Street, closes streets to create parks and new squares, widens pavements, enhances connections, better supports pedestrians and cyclists, and improves road safety. In doing so, it demonstrates public realm's potential as an antidote to some of the most pressing problems of today, including air quality, loneliness and climate breakdown.

Judges' comments: "We were impressed with the imagination of the scheme to put public health, well-being, sustainability, resilience, and time and space for reflection in the heart of London. This is a classic example of how through thoughtful landscape design, people can be nudged and supported to change behaviours and take time to enjoy their surroundings"

The Pineapple for Future Place

Winner: Port Loop, Birmingham – Urban Splash and Places for People
Port Loop is being transformed into a new family-focused, 43-acre waterside neighbourhood with more than 1,150 new homes, as well as commercial workspaces, parks, green spaces and community facilities that will include a new swimming pool. More than 1.5km of new towpaths will feature moorings, cycleways and walkways to the city, and even a waterbus stop.

Judges' comments:
"We felt the redevelopment of this inner-city, historic part of Birmingham, which juxtaposes respecting and reimagining the industrial heritage of the canal network, repurposed a vibrant and sustainable distinctive district in our second city"

The Pineapple for Place in Progress

Winner: London Dock, London – St George City, Patel Taylor
London Dock is a 6.2-hectare transformation of Wapping's historic docklands into a thriving urban district. A new grid of pathways, public squares and semi-private gardens draw people into the heart of the development and link the neighbourhood's spaces and buildings. Complementing this is an exemplary 1,800-home, mixed-use development, described by the press as a "game-changer" for Wapping.

Judges' comments: "Lovely scale, great historic reference, inviting, great use of landscape and water, and great connections"

The Pineapple for Place in Progress

Winner: Smith's Dock, North Shields – Urban Splash and Places for People
Smith's Dock is a former ship repair yard overlooking the River Tyne in North Shields. Steeped in heritage, the dock dates from the 1850s and closed in the late 1980s. The masterplan includes more than 800 homes of mixed tenure, as well as vast places to play, meaning anyone can find somewhere to be outside and enjoy life at Smith's Dock. Three dock inlets are a focal point – an ongoing symbol of the site's heritage.

Judges' comments:
"It captured industrial heritage with a good fishing and boat narrative, nice riverside path and skate park"

The Pineapple for Contribution to Place

Winner: Waltham Forest Walking and Cycling, London – London Borough of Waltham Forest
Waltham Forest is a diverse and vibrant place growing faster than any other London borough. To ensure this is sustainable, £27m of 'Mini-Holland' funding and £800,000 from Transport for London (Borough Cycling Programme) is being invested to improve infrastructure and encourage walking and cycling. The 'Enjoy Waltham Forest' programme focuses on a range of place-based development to ensure healthier lifestyles for all residents.

Judges' comments: "It was extraordinary to see how these multiple small projects created so much change for the public spaces of Waltham Forest. We all were blown away by how much was achieved: lots of things in a small way make the difference – not glamorous but effective for creating a place for the larger community"

The Pineapples – Finalists – Completed Place and Contribution to Place

London Wall Place, London –
Brookfield Properties and Oxford Properties,
Make Architects
The two new buildings on an important
historic site provide 46,500m² of office space
with nine roof terraces, accommodating
5,000 people and enclosing a public park.

One Tower Bridge, London –
Berkeley Homes and London Borough
of Southwark, Squire & Partners
Hotel and residential accommodation
supported by significant cultural, leisure,
restaurant and retail uses, including
The Bridge Theatre, as well as public realm.

Italian Gardens, Weston-super-Mare –
West of England Local Enterprise
Partnership, BDP
Linking the Italian Gardens with the town
square, the winter gardens pavilion provides
teaching and learning spaces, library, cafe,
restaurant and events space.

Merchant Square Footbridge, London –
European Land & Property,
Knight Architects
The replacement opening footbridge at
Paddington Basin spans 20m across the
Grand Union Canal.

Revealing the Charterhouse, London –
The Charterhouse, Eric Parry Architects
This Grade I listed complex of historic
buildings and gardens in the centre of London
has opened up part of its historic site to the
public for the first time in 650 years.

Television Centre, London –
Stanhope, Mitsui Fudosan, AIMCo and BBC
Studioworks, Allford Hall Monaghan Morris
Television Centre was the UK's first purpose-
built television studio and has been radically
reinvented as a new, mixed-use development.

The Department Store, London –
Squire & Partners
An unoccupied department store has been
reimagined to create inspiring workspaces,
units for local businesses, an event space and
two bars/restaurants.

The Pineapples – Finalists – Place in Progress

Battersea Power Station, London –
Battersea Power Station Development
Company
Circus West Village, the first of eight phases in
the development, is now open and abuzz, with
more than 1,100 people calling it home.

Blackwall Reach, London – Swan Housing
Association
Phase 1a has delivered 98 new affordable
homes, as well as a mosque, an extended local
school and a new community facility.

Broadgate, London – British Land, Arup
Plans to transform the complex from
a grey corporate fortress into a vibrant
neighbourhood include the creation of
five new buildings and a tripling of the
retail provision.

King's Cross, London – Argent
Already a lively place to visit day and night
with 50 new and repurposed buildings and a
mix of parks, streets, squares and gardens, the
project is due to complete in 2023.

Park Hill, Sheffield – Urban Splash and
Places for People
Phase 1 is complete with more than
260 homes, 30,000 sq ft of workspace, an
arts space, a nursery and a cafe.

Wembley Park, London – Quintain
With more than 1,750 homes, there is
also Wembley, London Designer Outlet,
Boxpark Wembley and Troubadour Wembley
Park Theatre.

The Pineapples – Finalists – Future Place

8 Albert Embankment, London –
U+I, Pilbrow & Partners
This major mixed-use masterplan on the site of the fire brigade's headquarters covers an area of 1.06 hectares and includes the creation of significant new areas of public realm.

Culture Mile, London – City of London
An initiative to transform the north-west corner of the Square Mile with a new cultural district, together with the Barbican, Guildhall School of Music & Drama, London Symphony Orchestra and the Museum of London.

Inner North West Masterplan, Belfast –
Belfast City Council
Currently underdeveloped and suffering from land-banking, Belfast City Council developed a masterplan with Feilden Clegg Bradley Studios to guide future development.

Kirkstall Forge, Leeds – CEG
A 57-acre, mixed-use scheme of 1,050 homes and 300,000 sq ft of high quality offices, leisure, shops and restaurants.

Oakfield, Swindon – Nationwide,
Metropolitan Workshop
Nationwide is trialling a new way to increase the UK's housing supply – delivering homes on zero profit from its CSR budget.

Temple, Leeds – CEG
This £350m development of an 8.69-acre brownfield site forms part of Leeds City Council's ambitious plan to double the size of the existing city centre.

The Chocolate Factory, London –
Haringey Council, Barton Willmore
Once the proud home of the Jelly Baby, this cluster has been claimed by creative industries and plans aim to build upon this.

Wickside, London – McGrath,
BUJ Architects
Transforms an industrial waste site with new roads, pedestrian linkages and permeability, while greatly reducing air pollution and providing facilities for canal communities.

The Festival of Place has been nominated for Event of the Year at the IBP awards in November

The need for trees: "They calm us down, they clean the air, they make us money"

Isabella Kaminski reports on the measurable economic benefits of tree-planting and why we need 1.5 billion more trees by 2050

Governments love a good tree-planting scheme, because they are popular and always hit the headlines. The latest source of funding, announced by former environment secretary Michael Gove in May, is a £10m pot available to councils, charities and individuals to plant 130,000 trees in towns and cities across England.

The money is certainly welcome. The UK has just 13% overall woodland cover – very low compared with most other European countries – and has made little progress in increasing it in recent years. The latest figures from Forest Research show only 1,420 hectares were planted in England in the year to March 2019, against the government's 5,000-hectare target, with smaller areas in Wales and Northern Ireland. Only Scotland met its goal, planting about 11,200 hectares.

But critics point out that, while 130,000 trees might sound a lot, it is only a drop in the metaphorical ocean. According to a recent Committee on Climate Change report, which emphasises the crucial role trees play in tackling climate change by storing carbon, we should be planting 30,000 hectares of woodland each year – equivalent to around 1.5bn trees by 2050.

Sharon Hosegood, chartered arboriculturist and consultant, says £10m is a good start "but it's obviously not enough. [There] needs to be a collaborative approach by the government, local government, developers and private individuals to pull together because we desperately need more trees".

This isn't a rural issue. Dan Raven-Ellison, who has campaigned to make London a National Park City, says the capital already has nearly as many trees as people, covering 21% of its area, but would like to see many more.

Trees have multiple benefits. Many of these can be quantified through a tool called i-Tree, which gives a detailed picture of the value of green infrastructure in cities such as London and Manchester.

As well as storing carbon, trees help counter the 'urban heat island' effect, whereby cities are warmer than rural areas. Wide-canopied trees provide physical shade and cooling in summer and warming in winter, which reduces the amount of energy needed for heating and air conditioning. This effect is more pronounced during heatwaves as the climate warms.

They also demonstrably improve air quality; large-leaved species in particular help reduce fine particulate pollution ($PM_{2.5}$). They boost biodiversity by providing homes for wildlife, reduce the risk of flooding by slowing down surface water run-off and improve soil health.

There is growing evidence that trees and other green spaces improve people's physical and mental health; a recent study found that a two-hour 'dose' of nature once a week significantly boosts well-being. And while money doesn't grow on trees they do have measurable economic benefits, boosting local house prices and encouraging trade by sprucing the area up.

"They calm us down, they clean the air, they make us money," summarises Hosegood. And mature trees do all these things better.

Hosegood says developers and councils are increasingly recognising these benefits. "In my work for a London local authority housing department there's a really good tree population and the landscaping has been greatly enhanced as part of privately funded development."

Part of the battle to increase the number of city trees is not to cut existing ones down. There are already significant barriers in place to doing this, with many trees protected by Tree Preservation Orders or within wider conservation areas.

Developers are restricted in what they can fell. Part of Hosegood's job involves assessing the state of existing trees on a development site, which is a statutory part of most planning applications. She looks at "how big they are, how healthy they are and what their role is in the landscape", in line with British Standard (BS) 5837.

"It's much better to get in early, preferably before the developer has bought the land, so we can work with the team – architects, landscape architects and engineers – to create a design that retains the best trees on site," says Hosegood. "There's always going to be some tree loss – that's inevitable – but if we can have a design that tries to keep the best trees and can mitigate the tree loss, that's really important."

Planting new trees is a whole different challenge and everyone agrees that there

---

UK's most valuable trees
According to a study by ShootGardening.co.uk with Tendercare in April, the following trees and plants can boost the value of UK property

1 Chinese magnolia: £8,500
2 Evergreen topiary: £1,900
3 Flowering cherry: £1,800
4 Evergreen magnolia grandiflora: £1,500
5 Cut-leaved purple Japanese maple: £1,200
6 Chinese windmill palm: £1,200
7 Olive: £500
8 Weeping birch: £300
9 Slow-growing hedge: £200/m
10 Camellia: £120

School children planting trees on industrial land in Manchester. Photo: Alamy

Greater Manchester's City of Trees project, which aims to grow the local tree population by at least three million within the next generation, has already planted half a million trees in a variety of locations, from large plots of urban woodland on the city's outskirts to pocket parks tucked between housing estates, to trees sprouting out of pavements

is no single correct way to do it. Greater Manchester's City of Trees project, which aims to grow the local tree population by at least three million within the next generation, has already planted half a million trees in a variety of locations; from large plots of urban woodland on the city's outskirts to pocket parks tucked between housing estates, to trees sprouting out of pavements.

Each type of planting has its own advantages and challenges. Parkland or woodland settings require considerably more land but once planted provide a more naturalistic landscape and may need less maintenance. Hard city landscapes also hugely benefit from greening, says Sarah Nurton, marketing and communications manager at City of Trees, but are particularly difficult to plant in.

Councils, highways organisations and nearby shopkeepers may need to be consulted about street trees, pavements must be wide enough to accommodate both the tree and passing foot traffic (including wheelchairs and buggies), and parking and entranceways cannot be obstructed. Meanwhile, some councils are concerned about insurance claims from subsidence caused by tree roots. "It is quite an expensive, time-consuming process and that's before you even get to digging up pavements and getting a tree in," says Nurton.

An important decision that developers and others must make is which species to plant. The Trees and Design Action Group (TDAG) produces a helpful free guide on this which is available online.

While there has been a move back towards native broadleaf trees such as oak in rural woodland, experts say these are not necessarily the best option in cities. Some woodland trees simply cannot be planted in urban locations. David Elliott, chief executive of tree planting charity Trees for Cities, says beech trees, for example, have very shallow roots that extend outwards, making them unsuitable for hard landscapes.

Meanwhile many native species are currently affected by serious pests and diseases, such as oak processionary moth and ash dieback disease. "The pool of our native species, which isn't that big anyway, is drastically reduced," says Elliott. "In order for trees to thrive and do well, to be healthy and resilient, the industry believes that you need to have a wide range of species."

Hosegood stresses that large-canopied trees are still important to maximise shade. "There was a tendency until recently for landscaping schemes to use smaller species with a smaller canopy because it was deemed safer and wouldn't give any trouble. There were fewer maintenance problems and it was cheaper," she says.

"But there's been a lot of lost opportunities. We need large trees where the space allows – things like London plane – but actually we need to be looking beyond our normal native trees because of climate change."

Changing climatic conditions means cities are becoming wetter during some parts of the year and drier and hotter at others. Nurton says City of Trees is considering which trees will survive the next 50 years and notes that some species are already being planted that would not have survived several decades ago. Paulownia – also known as the foxglove tree – is native to central and western China and can be killed by harsh winters but has thrived on St Peter's Square in Manchester city centre.

"It's about making our trees and woods

City of Trees is considering which trees will survive the next 50 years and notes that some species are already being planted that would not have survived several decades ago. The foxglove tree is native to central and western China and can be killed by harsh winters but has thrived on St Peter's Square in Manchester

more resilient for the future," says Nurton.

Another important consideration is what to plant trees in, because cities are bursting with buried infrastructure such as telecommunications cables, gas and water pipes and old building foundations.

"Developers need to think not just about the above-ground space but invest money in the below-ground space," says Hosegood. "What we've found in the past is that trees are sometimes just plonked in a hand-dug pit in the ground and left to get on with it. In a rural area that's absolutely fine. But in cities we have such competition for space underneath the ground [that] specialist tree pits are incredibly important."

A number of specialist suppliers sell modular systems that allow roots to flourish beneath hard surfaces and can maximise the water retention benefits of tree planting.

Julian Tollast, head of masterplanning and design at property development firm Quintain, which has won awards for its tree design at Wembley Park, says specialised technology is expensive but helps trees thrive, especially in the early years. Although Quintain generally favours watering trees manually with a hosepipe because "you know exactly what has been delivered", it has installed automatic irrigation systems underground in some areas.

Hosegood adds that, where possible, developers could plant several trees in one big pit rather than individually.

"You have a bigger soil volume for all the trees to exploit together. It's much better for surface water attenuation. It has a better visual impact and it's better ecologically as well because it's a more viable habitat for creepy crawlies etc. It seems like a cost... but I say it's really important because it'll make their development really shine when people go back."

Then there is the matter of long-term care. Hosegood says it is helpful when planning permission includes maintenance conditions specifying how trees are to be looked after for a fixed period, often five years. This is usually done by a maintenance company, contracted by the council or the developer itself.

At Wembley Park, however, Quintain remains responsible for the site. "We took a long-term stewardship of the landscape we're creating," says Tollast, "which really helps because I can chat to my colleague, learn from the last area of landscape we did on the challenges or otherwise we've had of maintaining that and make sure we put those lessons learned back into the next phase of the project."

Trees for Cities looks after its new street trees for three years after they are handed over to the landowner – usually

Avenue of trees along Salford Quays. Photo: Alamy

the local authority. Elliott says most trees aged between three and 20 years do not require a lot of work. "Then when they're bigger you start to need to do pruning or pollarding or take them down if they're starting to die off," he says.

Progressive developers are even involving the public in the installation and long-term care of their trees. Elliott of Trees for Cities, which relies on a mostly voluntary workforce to create its urban woodlands, community orchards, leafy parks and street greenery, says local communities that plant trees "will take more ownership and care for them".

Hosegood says getting communities involved is also "an opportunity for developers to show they're different from their competitors and to show their green credentials". Having children plant trees on a construction site is "tremendous education and it's great for PR", while making community groups responsible for longer-term management of nearby woodland is "a mechanism for the new people who are moving in to get to know each other".

It is also important because trees can be an emotive subject. Protests erupted in Sheffield in 2016 when contractor Amey started felling street trees as part of a 25-year private finance initiative contract with the city council.

For Elliott, a good tree-planting project

is one that maximises its benefits, so he welcomes the fact that the Urban Tree Challenge Fund prioritises social factors as well as environmental ones.

Nurton, who often works with social housing providers, says they are particularly enthusiastic about the idea of greening patches of land that might have attracted anti-social behaviour. "If we can bring that woodland back into use for the community, we might twin it with a local school. They use it as an outdoor classroom so it's much less likely to get fly-tipped and people see it as an asset rather than an eyesore. They really see the value of that."

Elliott thinks there is still a lack of consistency in how green infrastructure is approached in different areas and says it is not completely embedded in the wider planning and development sector. "But there is a rapidly increasing [realisation] of the value of green in urban development. It is being taken much more seriously."

He hopes that a new requirement for developers in England to show that projects have a positive impact or 'net gain' for biodiversity will improve things further.

Nurton agrees. "When it comes to costs... it can be hard to prioritise green space and trees within developments, which we completely understand. But I think it's becoming more and more integral now

for developers to ensure that it's one of the strands.

"It's not just about building flats; it's about creating environments people want to be in."

Isabella Kaminski is an environmental journalist. Follow her on Twitter @Isabella_Kam

How Miami is shoring itself up

Reworking the budget through the lens of resilience has revolutionised the way Miami is developing. Chris Stokel-Walker reports on the 59 ways they are building a better county

A weather reporter illustrates the force of the winds caused by Hurricane Irma as it arrives in Miami in 2017. Photo: Getty

Miami is flat, low-lying, surrounded by rising seas and built on porous limestone with tiny holes through which sea water rises. Photo: Getty

In 100 cities around the world, including Britain's Belfast, Bristol, Glasgow, Manchester and London, a raft of bureaucrats are planning for the future. Sat alongside mayors and councillors, they are trying to tackle the multifaceted, competing challenges that will face cities in the decades to come.

The post of chief resilience officer (CRO) is largely an invention of The Rockefeller Foundation, which in 2013 instigated a programme, 100 Resilient Cities, to improve cities across the globe and their ability to respond to the changing environment.

"It was built on a lot of the work they'd been doing about climate adaptation over the course of a decade-plus, largely in response to three main drivers: urbanisation, globalisation and climate change," explains Peter Jenkins, senior programme manager for city resilience delivery in North America at 100 Resilient Cities.

The foundation was set up to fund cities to employ CROs who could help them understand the greatest risks to their future – and do something about it.

100 Resilient Cities was a response to the havoc that Hurricanes Katrina and Sandy wreaked on US cities, as well as an acknowledgement that the way we live is changing – and becoming more precarious. Global warming is a serious risk to our way of life.

"It requires new types of thinking, and new structures around planning, decision-making and urban governance, to be able to better address those challenges in integrated ways," says Jenkins. "That's what the programme ultimately sought to accomplish." Hundreds of applications were received over the course of the three rounds of the programme, with 100 cities making the cut.

But in April this year, the president of The Rockefeller Foundation announced to staff that 100 Resilient Cities would close. There were rumours that a change in leadership at the foundation had caused the shift, and

"It's interesting that Resilient305 incorporates a lot of activities that were previously happening in the region but is floundering or not receiving the real support of leadership. The hope was bringing them under the Resilient305 label would give them a bit more life"

worries that support would be withdrawn from the participating cities and CROs left to wither on the vine.

The Rockefeller Foundation has announced a grant to the Atlantic Council to support the resilient cities and will continue to help their CROs to share best practices worldwide. However, at the time we spoke, Jenkins was preparing to leave his post.

Miami is one city committed to ensuring the impact of 100 Resilient Cities lives on, even as the initial initiative shuts up shop. Carlos Martin, senior fellow at the Urban Institute, a non-profit organisation brought in to analyse the impact of the 100 Resilient Cities initiative, says there is a simple explanation for this.

"Miami is one of those places that realised their days are limited unless they act immediately."

(However, it is worth noting that Florida's former governor, Rick Scott, used to expunge any mention of 'climate change' or 'global warming' from official documents. That stopped in January 2019 with the swearing in of new governor Ron DeSantis.)

Nichole Hefty, deputy resilience officer at Miami-Dade County's Department of Regulatory and Economic Resources, explains: "We initially went into this focusing on our specific challenges with regards to climate change and sea-level rise."

Workers board up Mango's restaurant and nightclub in preparation for an approaching hurricane. Photo: Getty

Miami-Dade County and the cities of Miami and Miami Beach, which applied together as a partnership for the 100 Resilient Cities programme, expect sea levels to rise between one and two feet from 1992 levels by 2060. That could have deleterious effects on the community, ranging from saltwater poisoning the sources of drinking water in the region to flooded buildings near the coast and waterlogged roads. Florida also sees "more than its fair share" of hurricanes, says Hefty. All of this requires thinking to bounce back from.

But the development of a document outlining all the risks and concerns – termed 'stresses' and 'shocks' in the parlance of CROs – allowed the Miami project, now christened Resilient305 after the telephone dialling code for the area, to highlight other areas of concern.

Its future-proofing strategy is divided into three main areas, says Sara McTarnaghan, research associate at the Urban Institute, who has investigated the Resilient305 project.

"It's organised around 'places', which deals with a lot of the environmental risk; 'people', which deals with a lot of the socio-economic opportunity; and 'pathways', which is an interesting area and quite unique from other strategies – it's how do they do regional governance on this issue," she says.

One of the reasons for CROs is to break down the silos in government and make people work more in partnership – as evidenced by the fact the Resilient305 plan caters for two cities, a county and 32 other municipalities.

Hefty says: "We quickly realised while climate is certainly a challenge for us, we have a lot of long-term challenges we really could benefit from working more collaboratively on. Some of the other stresses that are chronic challenges to our community are transportation and affordable housing, and we have certain areas that are in extreme poverty."

The three partners spent a year identifying the gaps that needed to be filled with the development of a resilience strategy. They went into the community, asked residents – even some who didn't fall under the auspices of either city – what they felt needed improving, convened gatherings of experts and conducted online surveys.

She says: "Some of these things we and other communities have been trying to address and improve for a long period of time and it seems like some of these challenges – despite the fact you've got resources devoted to them and people working on them – can be hard to get beyond a certain plateau. We took the time to identify some of those things that needed to be changed, to be done differently, or to better connect the

dots in order to move the needle on some of these challenges."

What resulted was a list of 59 actions the area needed to do to guarantee its future. Jenkins says this is remarkable and unprecedented: "Resilient305 is a single document, a single vision, that has been endorsed. This then enabled them to work with the other municipalities, which were invited to sign onto the strategy."

The document tackles the bigger challenges, including global warming and the risks associated with that and an attempt to engage the community in ways that feel more inclusive, as well as more fundamental shifts. Hefty says: "We're looking at, for example, a platform on which we can better co-ordinate our utility work."

Miami-Dade County's water and sewer department has a long-term programme to improve its infrastructure, aimed at alleviating some of the stresses on the system in the aftermath of hurricanes and associated flooding. But as any city dweller knows, municipal repair teams often don't talk to each other. The sewerage team can dig up the road one year to fix the underground system and the next year the municipality's roadworks team comes along to tear up the tarmac to repair a pavement.

"We're looking at using some online platforms and existing working groups to better co-ordinate that type of work, so there's less disruption in operations and in the community, and efficiencies in cost and workforce that are used," says Hefty.

Through the establishment of CROs, the greater Miami area has been able to develop new projects and improve existing ones. The area's history with hurricanes means its Office of Emergency Management is seen as a leader in the field, but the resilience programme has allowed it to improve its preparation and services for underserved communities.

One programme being expanded through the Resilient305 plan is the Community Emergency Response Team, which helps to identify vulnerable individuals who cannot prepare for natural disasters because they lack the money or transport.

McTarnaghan explains: "It's interesting that Resilient305 incorporates a lot of activities that were previously happening in the region but is floundering or not receiving the real support of leadership. The hope was bringing them under the Resilient305 label would give them a bit more life. That's especially true for some of the stuff on the income-inequality side."

Hefty adds: "What we're really doing is making sure not only are we co-ordinating it at a county level, but we're continuing to work with our non-profits and other sector leaders in the community, not only to keep these issues current but to continue to make progress.

"We all get very busy with the different things we do every day and this is a long-term strategy and process. Some of the projects we expect to complete within a year, but others we expect will take more than five years."

Resilient305 has involved a fundamental shift in the way things are organised by the greater Miami area's government.

"For the first time, our county budget is now organised around the four pillars of resilience, as identified by the Rockefeller 100 Resilient Cities programme," explains Sandra St Hilaire, resilience co-ordinator at Miami-Dade County.

Miami-Dade Emergency Operations Center

"We have a lot of long-term challenges we really could benefit from working more collaboratively on. Chronic challenges to our community are transportation and affordable housing, and we have certain areas that are in extreme poverty"

She adds: "Having our Office of Management and Budget shift that work through the lens of resilience has really revolutionised the way Miami-Dade County is thinking about resilience and building it into all our county operations."

While 100 Resilient Cities may disappear, Resilient305 will not. Hefty says: "It's up to us to make sure we are continually out there, working with our stakeholders, to not only maintain the progress but to keep it relevant.

"We know things change, but we also know this is a live document. As priorities change, we may need to tweak to continue that progress forward."

Find out more
www.100resilientcities.org
resilient305.com

Resilient305's 59 actions
1 Preserve and restore Biscayne Bay
2 Build reef biodiversity and defences
3 Bolster our beaches
4 Expand nature-based infrastructure
5 Integrate resilience into open spaces
6 Reduce 'back-bay' flooding
7 Implement sea level rise strategy
8 Develop sea level rise checklist for capital projects
9 Create development review checklist
10 Strengthen resilience planning
11 Maximise opportunity zones
12 Develop mobility hubs in the 305
13 Design a better bus network
14 Drive into the future
15 It's electric
16 Expand renewable energy
17 Building Efficiency 305
18 Stay and live in the 305
19 Redeveloping resilient public housing
20 Build an inclusive economy
21 Train for construction
22 Promote fair-chance hiring
23 Buy local
24 Be counted
25 Re-establish the financial capability collaborative
26 Teach kids to save
27 Expand youth career opportunities
28 Break the cycle of youth violence
29 Respect our elders
30 Update the social services masterplan
31 Advocate for mental health
32 Pilot an arrest diversion for opioid users
33 Accelerate HIV/AIDS strategy
34 Advance pandemics communication
35 Increase neighbourhood response
36 Time to volunteer
37 Prepare your property
38 Support resilience hubs
39 Get the 311 on resilience for the 305
40 Create a K-12 plan for resilience literacy
41 See it to believe it
42 Pre-planning for post-disaster toolkit
43 Roll-out guide to recovery financing
44 Bounce forward 305 – distribute resilient urban land use essentials guide
45 Send your boss to bootcamp
46 Resilient 35 in the 305 network
47 Train employees to be resilient
48 Rise to the rescue
49 Collaborate with universities
50 Create a science advisory panel
51 Resilience accelerator workshops
52 Create a Resilient305 ArcGIS hub
53 Share bold integrated water models
54 Employ a one-water approach
55 Plan efficiently and effectively together
56 Finance a resilient future
57 Leverage the power of purchasing
58 Pilot resilience financing toolkit
59 Demonstrate cost benefits of resilience

Trees and other infrastructure are vulnerable to storm damage. Photo: Getty

Storm-water pumps will help to stop rising sea levels from inundating low-lying areas. Photo: Getty

Why northern cities are battling to front the cycling and walking peloton

What is behind this desire to turn Sheffield, Liverpool and Manchester into Amsterdam-style cycling paradises? Will it work? And what could it mean for developers? James Wilmore reports

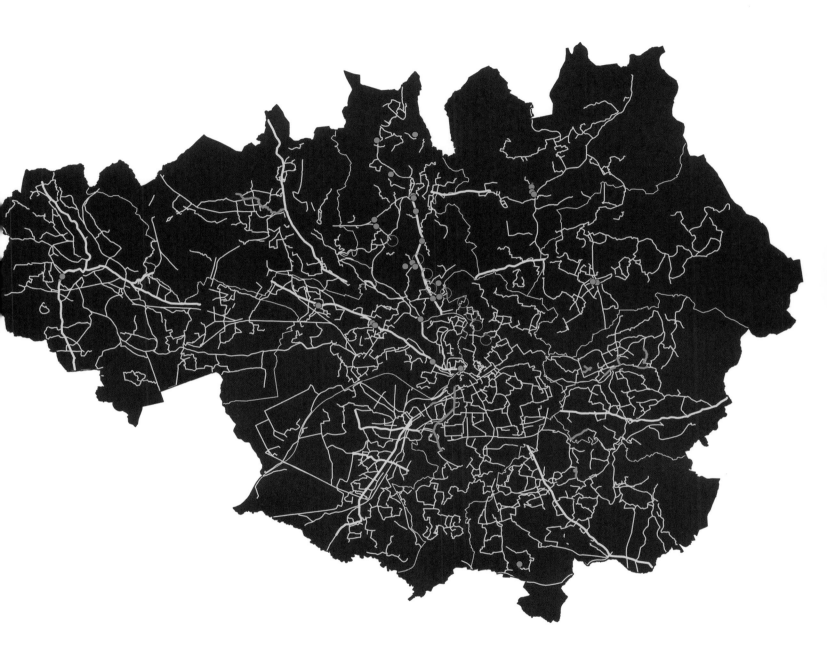

The plan for Greater Manchester's cycling and walking network, known as Beelines, from July 2018. The green lines represent confirmed cycle paths, dots are crossing points and junction upgrades, green circles are cycle parking at Metrolink stations, yellow lines are proposed cycle paths and thick yellow lines are proposed with full segregation and public realm improvements

Andy Burnham had a shock on day one as Labour's then newly appointed health secretary. Brimming with a plan to push physical activity for good health, he marched in to discuss it with his new colleagues. The idea, however, fell on deaf ears.

"I remember saying... that the promotion of physical activity should be core business for the department," the Liverpool-born politician told a parliamentary select committee in March 2019. "They looked at me as if I was speaking a foreign language."

Fast forward a decade and as mayor of Greater Manchester, Burnham's zeal still burns. While his initial progress at the Department of Health was thwarted, one of his first acts as mayor was installing former Olympic cyclist Chris Boardman as his cycling tsar. Between them, they have ambitious plans to turn Greater Manchester into a cycling nirvana.

Manchester, however, has neighbouring competition at the front of the peloton. Across the Peak District, Sheffield mayor Dan Jarvis appointed Paralympian Dame Sarah Storey as his new walking and cycling commissioner in April as the region ramps up infrastructure spending plans. Meanwhile, Manchester's great rival, Liverpool, also unveiled its first active travel commissioner this year amid plans to boost its cycling network.

So, what is behind this desire to turn cities into Amsterdam-style cycling paradises? Will it work? And what could it mean for developers?

Two years ago, the Department for Transport launched a 'Cycling and Walking Investment Strategy'. Page one of that document spelt out the aim: "We want to make cycling and walking the natural choices for shorter journeys, or as part of a longer journey."

Inside, the document expanded: "For too long, some have seen cycling as a niche activity, rather than a normal activity for all. If we can increase levels of walking and

Aerial view of Stockport Interchange and the cycling and walking bridge. Photo: Transport for Greater Manchester

Dan Jarvis, mayor of Sheffield

cycling, the benefits are substantial." Cheaper travel, better health, lower congestion, better air quality, and "vibrant, attractive places and communities", are all listed as benefits.

The UK could certainly do with a push in these areas. Seven out of 10 UK adults never ride a bike, yet the UK has Europe's third-highest obesity rate. The UK is the world's 10th most congested country. And more than 40 of UK towns and cities are at, or have exceeded, air pollution limits set by the World Health Organization.

Part of the problem lies in the deep-rooted suspicion around cyclists: a them-and-us attitude between people who sometimes choose to travel on two wheels and committed motorists. Social media is full of videos of angry exchanges between car drivers and cyclists battling it out on Britain's roads. It is a depressing spectacle, especially compared to the normality of cycling in more progressive European countries, such as the Netherlands and Denmark.

In Manchester, where pollution levels have been branded a "public health crisis", the need is greater than most.

Martin Key, an advisor to Boardman at the Greater Manchester Combined Authority, believes this problem can be overcome. "We have to normalise the activity, and that means properly catering for people," he says. "In London, you see lots of different people riding bikes and that's because of the infrastructure."

Safety, however, remains the key concern for many. Key says around 60% of people would consider active modes of transport if they felt safe, according to research.

The Manchester city region has created an overall £1.5bn masterplan, involving building 70 miles of new cycling and walking routes, known as the Bee Network. Last month, a second wave of proposals were unveiled, allocating another £137m on the plans, including a radical cycling and walking bridge in Stockport.

Key believes there is little choice, with an unprecedented amount of development exploding across the city centre.

"As the city grows, we have got to get people to travel in different ways," explains

Key. "Cycling's not for every journey, it's about shifting a small number of journeys."

And this is where developers come in. "I really hope the scale of the [Beelines] network inspires developers," says Key. "It will change the look and feel [of the city], increase house prices and the desire for people to drive their car all the time."

One developer that is already embracing the changes is Manchester-based Capital & Centric. On two of its residential sites in Manchester – Crusader Mill and Talbot – it is developing the spaces without car parks and replacing them with courtyards and cycle parking spaces.

"It's a change of approach," says Adam Higgins, co-founder at Capital & Centric. "It felt like a brave decision a few years ago and we wondered if we were going to get support of other planners."

But now, Higgins thinks the move makes total sense. "With driverless cars, the continuing rise of car clubs and fewer young people driving, car parking is becoming less and less relevant. It's a complete backward step to be putting a car park in the middle of what could be a beautiful residents' garden."

In fact, he argues it is essential that as Manchester's city centre population soars, deterring cars and encouraging cycling and walking becomes a priority.

"If all those new people had cars, Manchester would become a deeply unpleasant place to live," says Higgins. "We don't want to become like London. As its population increases, Manchester needs to learn from London's mistakes over traffic."

In Sheffield, Capital & Centric is adopting a similar approach. Its 97-loft apartment development, Eyewitness, is also being built without a car park. Higgins is encouraged by the response so far from buyers.

Author, architect and cycling advocate Steven Fleming agrees that developers should be brave in their approach.

"The fear is that rich people aren't going to want to come and buy, so you're going to lose out," he says. But he points to a scheme he advised on in Australia, where the sale price of apartments actually doubled, partly due to incorporating cycle storage.

When it comes to convincing people to cycle in Sheffield though, the city has a particular challenge – its hills. Even Dame Sarah has admitted the Steel City has some "crazy hills".

But Mark Lynam, director of programme commissioning at Sheffield City Region, argues the problem of hills can be overcome. "They are something we need to consider, but should not be used as an excuse," he says. "It's about working smartly on how we design the infrastructure."

Chorlton Cycleway, Brooks Bar Junction. Image: Transport for Greater Manchester

Lynam believes forward-thinking developers are embracing these changes in the Sheffield region, but urges more to come on board. "We can't afford to be building housing or office developments that do not take into account increasingly people's desire to have greater choices over how they travel," he says. "We've seen developers building new offices with shower facilities. But there's not enough of it, it needs to become the norm rather than the exception."

In Liverpool, the ambition is equally great. Last December, metro mayor Steve Rotheram revealed work is set to start on the first phase of a "potential" new 373-mile walking and cycling network for the region. "We want people across the city region to work with us to develop ideas to get more people cycling and walking more, so the network we develop is built for them," said

"I remember saying that the promotion of physical activity should be core business for the department. They looked at me as if I was speaking a foreign language'

Mr Rotheram. But he admitted: "We can't transform the situation overnight."

Jayne Rodgers, Liverpool's new cycling and walking officer, says the city has the advantage of already having lots of green spaces. "We are looking at how we can improve linkages to the parks and how that fits in with the existing cycle network," she says in an upbeat YouTube clip.

The activity in these three cities, and plenty more across the North and the rest of the UK, shows no shortage of ambition. The key thing will be securing on-going cash to pay for the projects.

At the transport select committee hearing in March, Boardman voiced his frustration at the piecemeal funding approach by central government. "We are devoting lumps of cash to it, as and when we can find it, and it is absolutely crazy. Whatever mechanism it is, it needs consistent prioritising and funding," he said.

Burnham even suggested the Department of Health should be asked to fund cycling infrastructure as it can help save money in the long term, returning to his theme from a decade earlier.

Burnham added: "My simple point is that cycling and walking should be treated in the exactly same way as road investment – it needs a long-term, national, significant funding stream."

Fleming echoes this point. "Let's not fund cycling infra from the crumbs we use on park benches and tennis courts," he says.

But, despite being the author of a book called *Velotopia*, Fleming adds a dose of realism: "Everybody is stuck with the cost of a car, congestion, fumes and traffic deaths," he says.

"It's a mad system, but the capacity has been built for it. Driving is going to stay very popular and mainstream for a long time to come."

James Wilmore is a business journalist and editor with 15 years' experience of working for national and global B2B titles, including Retail Week, Construction News, Just Drinks, The Publican and Inside Housing

"Developers can no longer get away with sticking trees in concrete"

The government's paper on biodiversity net gain, published in July, places greater onus on developers to restore the environment when building new schemes. Anna White reports

Cities in the UK are caught in a web of interwoven crises: the critical decline of ecosystems is compounded by the affordable housing shortage and climate emergency.

Paul de Zylva, a Friends of the Earth campaigner, sums it up. "Rising temperatures are causing soil erosion and eradication of habitats, and we swing between drought and flood. On this land we continue to hurriedly build more homes rather than true sustainable communities with a sense of place and permanence."

The government's paper on biodiversity net gain, published in July following a 10-week industry consultation, is an attempt to put greater onus on the development community to protect and restore the natural environment when building new schemes.

It includes a new metric from the Department for Environment, Food and Rural Affairs (Defra) to quantify the ecology output by developers.

The response – to be subsumed into the Draft Environment Bill – was muffled by the noise surrounding the appointment of Boris Johnson as Conservative Party leader and prime minister, but needs rigorous analysis.

It will get this treatment at *The Developer's* Risk & Resilience Conference on Friday 8 November at the Science Museum, London, when the development industry and conservation experts assess the impact and up-take of the new guidelines.

Biodiversity net gain seeks to ensure that when delivering commercial, residential and mixed-use schemes developers improve the environment, not just compensating for the biodiversity loss when concreting over habitats, but increasing their number.

"Biodiversity net gain requires developers to ensure habitats for wildlife are enhanced and left in a measurably better state than they were pre-development," explains Alex Green, sustainability director at the British Property Federation (BPF).

"Developers must assess the type of habitats and their condition before submitting plans, and then demonstrate how they are improving biodiversity – through actions such as the creation of green corridors, by planting more trees or forming local nature spaces"

"Developers must assess the type of habitats and their condition before submitting plans, and then demonstrate how they are improving biodiversity – through actions such as the creation of green corridors, by planting more trees or forming local nature spaces."

It is not a massive departure from recent procedure, Green continues, and planning permission is contingent on green compensation. But new proposals will take this a step further.

"It's no longer enough to mitigate. Now the industry must ecologically enhance a site," he says.

The consultation solicited responses from the development industry, conservation community, planners and the public on updating Defra's biodiversity net gain metric.

The government describes it as "designed to provide ecologists, developers, planners and other interested parties with a means of assessing changes in biodiversity value (losses or gains) brought about by development or changes in land management. The metric is a habitat-based approach to determining a proxy biodiversity value".

The revised metric includes the following new features: improved consideration of ecological connectivity, an extended range of habitat types including green infrastructure and rivers, and a forthcoming spreadsheet-based tool which will support the application of the metric in practice.

"Before any plans are made, the biodiversity score of a site is taken. Plans must then set out ways the developer can increase the ecological content of the site by a minimum of 10%," Green explains.

The BPF is supportive of the proposals: "It provides an opportunity to consistently know what is required of the developer who wants to know where they stand with planning," he adds.

De Zylva believes it is a micro-step in the right direction. "Public mood is changing, we are becoming more disparaging of schemes with low natural value. Developers can no longer get away with sticking trees in concrete and laying turf, and through biodiversity net gain there's a chance to incentivise the right behaviours."

He commends the UK government for attempting to enshrine biodiversity net gain (or "the son of offsetting") in law but says: "On this subject that's as generous as I am going to get."

Only 8% of respondents to the consultation were developers – the majority were planners and conservation campaigners – but Taylor Wimpey argued against an update to the metric. The volume house builder was concerned that biodiversity

Australia Road, White City, London – community needs are integrated with surface water management, resulting in a safe, car-free route to school

Dedicated highways enable hedgehogs to cross otherwise dangerous areas without risk of harm. Photo: Andrea Ormesby

was being elevated above other planning considerations.

"It is not clear why biodiversity should be made mandatory and hence elevated above other important social and environmental priorities. We therefore cannot support the mandatory aspect of the consultation," the formal response reads.

Developer Redrow was also involved in the consultation. "A 10% target has been proposed but it hasn't yet been made fully clear why the government has settled on this figure. Some of our schemes have seen significant net gains by as much as 60% but others will not be as high. In the absence of robust evidence we feel 5% is a more appropriate target in which to start, reviewing this, as appropriate, as the industry gains experience," says Nicola Johansen, its group sustainability manager.

Redrow has taken a proactive approach, forming corporate partnerships with The Wildlife Trusts and the Bumblebee Conservation Trust to introduce a variety of pollination-friendly measures, bat bricks, bird boxes and hedgehog highways.

"Redrow is working in partnership with The Wildlife Trusts to create a new biodiversity strategy that will include achieving biodiversity net gains. Our new strategy will go beyond net gain in that it will seek to ensure that enhancements are made in a way that is relevant to the local landscape's character and considers local species," says Johansen.

The Saxon Brook development in Exeter is forecast to achieve net gains of 15%, partly due to the planting of species-rich wildflower meadows, native woodland including a community orchard, new ponds with emergent and marginal vegetation and marshy grassland.

The Chartered Institute of Ecology and Environmental Management (CIEEM) criticised the 10% minimum gain requirement: "This is disappointing as a 10% gain measured over time may still result in a loss of biodiversity due to the ongoing decline and the reality that some biodiversity net gain projects will simply not succeed. Local authorities will have the ability to be more ambitious, but we will have to see if they do so given their continued under-resourcing."

The House Builders Association (HBA), typically representing smaller development organisations, supported the metric but said: "There should be efforts made to simplify certain sized/types of sites so that smaller house builders are not subject to long delays and costly assessments."

At first glance, the proposals should level an uneven playing field. Chris Brown is the founder of Igloo Regeneration – an ethical developer that 'makes profit for purpose'.

He believes the ecological assessment of a site has for too long been easily manipulated by the larger players.

"The big boys can afford to hire a consultant who can tell them what they want to hear regarding the biodiversity of the site and bend the ecology report to planners," he says. In theory, the metric system – which seems relatively straightforward – should give a more consistent and measurable approach.

However, he's unconvinced. "The perception of the small and medium-sized developer will be that this is yet another barrier to entry, another one of an increasingly long list of things they need to tick off for planning," he says.

New guidance was needed to address the "patchwork" of different approaches to greenwashing, says de Zylva, but the government's response could create confusion as every local authority planning body interprets it differently.

"It's near impossible to work out the net gain/loss without an ecologist and then they just argue with the local authority ecologist. The value of greenfield is so subjective," says a source from a national house builder.

Prior to 23 July the industry was expecting a hierarchy system. The first expectation was that the developer would leave the site in a better ecological state than when it was acquired. If there were restrictions on the site, the second requirement was that the developer and planner could agree that this environmental contribution could be made elsewhere. If this was not possible then the third and final resort was the payment of a levy to the local authority to cover habitat creation locally.

Much to the surprise of the BPF, the tariff was dropped in the response – deemed too complicated to enforce but potentially rendering the mechanism toothless.

The response reads: "The government will not introduce a new tariff on loss of biodiversity. By not instating a rigid tariff mechanism, government will make it easier for local authorities, landowners and organisations to set up habitat compensation schemes locally where they wish to do so."

This will give each council the freedom to devise their own compensation schemes which could vary widely, and potentially cost the developer more in fees to agree upon compensation and dispute resolution than the tariff itself.

One county or city council may have a more favourable approach over another, driving inconsistent levels of housebuilding in different parts of the country with an inevitable impact on local pricing and residents.

There are also exemptions, namely small sites and brownfield. "Small sites will remain in scope of the mandate, but consideration will be given to whether minor residential developments should be subject to longer transition arrangements or a lower net gain requirement than other types of development," explains Green.

"There will be a targeted exemption for brownfield sites that meet a number of criteria including that they do not contain priority habitats or if they face genuine difficulties in delivering viable development."

However, in London the vast majority of large residential schemes are former industrial brownfield transformations.

As Brown explains: "Ninety-eight per

"Ninety-eight per cent of previously developed land in London scores a zero on the biodiversity net gain metric so will require very little ecological input. This low-level biodiversity net gain does not even start us on the journey to rewild London"

cent of previously developed land in London scores a zero on the biodiversity net gain metric so will require very little ecological input. This low-level biodiversity net gain does not even start us on the journey to rewild London."

De Zylva agrees: "Nature is on the brink. The fact that once-common birds such as starlings are now on the endangered list tells us how intense the ecosystems crisis has become."

Further consultation is underway on marine sites, deemed too complex to be wrapped into this paper, and large infrastructure projects have been excluded, too.

CIEEM had this to say: "We are extremely disappointed that nationally significant infrastructure projects (NSIPs) will remain outside of the scope of mandatory biodiversity net gain. NSIPs are at a scale that they have disproportionately large impacts on the natural environment. They should be seen by government as an opportunity to lead the way in delivering biodiversity net gain and in realising the ambition of leaving the environment in a better state than we inherited it."

The current political landscape is highly relevant to the natural one. Over the course of the UK's prolonged period of austerity, planning departments have suffered staff cuts, and therefore a local authority's ability to ensure each site is assessed properly, thoroughly read site reports and devise their own compensation schemes is a tall order.

On 5 August, the HM Treasury report *Public Expenditure Statistical Analyses 2019* was published and revealed an increase in the Defra budget of £213m to day-to-day spend of £2.16bn. Much is being spent on increased administration and salary costs due to Brexit preparation. And yet, funds for the protection of the landscape and biodiversity continue to fall and have halved since 2016/17.

"The dramatic decline in funding for landscape and biodiversity is at odds with the government's stated ambitions in its 25-Year Environment Plan to restore biodiversity and recognise the value of nature to our social and economic well-being," CIEEM complains.

For de Zylva the updated metric and biodiversity net gain proposals do not go far enough. "The government is pulling a distracting lever rather than focusing on the intensive and radical restoration of nature that is needed," he says. "We need a comprehensive plan from government to reverse the ecosystem emergency," he concludes.

The absence of a far-reaching and cohesive strategy and the perception that Brexit will delay the Draft Environment Bill

Pollination-friendly planting at Caddington Woods development near Luton

means some developers are dismissive of the incoming legislation.

"It's not something we are concerned with at the moment," the boss of a small house builder tells *The Developer*, referring to biodiversity net gain.

Yes, they are sensitive to the environment in which they are building. Yes, they plan to preserve the existing habitat and build around it as much as possible. But this particular developer – which specialises in small luxury boutique residential schemes in south-west London – is not as yet required by law to put back on to the site more ecology than they bought it with.

When that changes, they might find the government's new guidance leaves them with more questions than answers.

Anna White is a journalist, copywriter and communications consultant. She was head of property at the Telegraph Media Group and has worked for KPMG, PricewaterhouseCoopers and Ernst & Young

Find out more
tinyurl.com/DefraBiodiversity

From drain to sponge city

We need to 'depave' our cities, street by street, says De Urbanisten's Dirk van Peijpe, whose famous water squares combine climate resilience with public space. Christine Murray reports

"How do we deal with this climate crisis and can we do it in such a way that we also create spaces that add value to the community and their quality of life?" asks Dirk van Peijpe, founder of Rotterdam urban design studio, De Urbanisten.

We're talking about De Urbanisten's Water Square project in Rotterdam, which famously doubles up flood-proofing with public space. But van Peijpe could be summing up the challenge facing city leaders across the UK.

Fresh evidence shows sea levels are rising at an unprecedented rate, and the latest report from the UN's Intergovernmental Panel on Climate Change found that by 2050, those one-in-100-year weather events could happen every year, unless the global population dramatically curbs emissions.

It is a scary statistic when you realise that 10% of all new homes built in England in 2016-17 were constructed in type three flood zones with a "one in 100 or greater annual probability of river flooding", including 53% of all new homes built in Newham and 48% of those in North Somerset. And the rate at which the UK is building homes on the floodplain is accelerating.

As a result, there has been a rise in planning rejections for schemes that do not include flood-proofing by design.

These are set to increase further with new requirements that force developments to reduce run-off from cloudbursts with features such as swales.

In Hull, where 98% of all homes are at high risk of flooding, the inclusion of sustainable drainage systems (SuDS) in all new developments is now legally binding. Wales has also made SuDS inclusion mandatory.

Other local authorities are prioritising sustainable drainage in line with the National Planning Policy Framework, which stipulates that SuDS should be given first preference in development plans. New guidelines coming into effect in April 2020 with Sewage for Adoption 8 will also see planning authorities updating their policies to align with new Ofwat standards.

Now, with flooding hitting the headlines after a seasonal drought in London, plus the recent climate strikes and the growing public clamour for greener cities with less toxic air, it is understandable that water excess and shortage, air quality and biodiversity have rocketed up the planning agenda.

Rotterdam, on the other hand, has been facing the threat of floods for hundreds of years, so the city is ahead of the UK when it comes to innovation in urban water solutions. As such, its designers are also sought after as leaders in water-sensitive design – one of the reasons van Peijpe, by popular demand, has been invited to present his work at The Developer Live: Risk & Resilience conference on 8 November in London.

Although it has been five years since De Urbanisten celebrated the opening of Benthemplein, its first water square, delegations still enthusiastically visit this once-empty public space every year.

When dry, which is 90% of the time, its three basins serve as basketball and skateboarding courts. During a cloudburst or flash flood, the water is filtered before it enters the square and runs out of spouts and along gutters until it fills the play courts, which become water collection ponds. The water is retained for a day or two until it drains into the ground or is pumped into a nearby canal.

"The critical point is that none of the water goes into the sewers," says van Peijpe.

The concept was borne out of what van Peijpe calls "our first wake-up call to climate change", in 2006, following the publication of Al Gore's *An Inconvenient Truth*.

Rotterdam had been investing in expensive underground rainwater tanks to prevent the overwhelming of the sewage system. De Urbanisten's idea was to take these technical drainage projects and combine them with a public space need in dense neighbourhoods.

One benefit to this was the opportunity to combine the city's wastewater budget with a public space grant.

"When you can link it to other programmes and needs, you can stack your budget," says van Peijpe. "Sixty per cent of the finance was paid out of funding dedicated to sewage renewal, with 40% of the budget linked to city beautification."

This holistic approach is the hallmark of 'resilience', a concept encouraged by movements such as the Rockefeller Foundation's 100 Resilient Cities project, founded on the idea that city budgets for maintenance and upgrades could be combined with the need for environmental improvements.

When it rains, the basketball and skateboarding courts become water collection ponds. The water is retained for a day or two until it drains into the ground or is pumped into a nearby canal

Benthemplein water square in Rotterdam combines water storage with improving the quality of urban public space. Photo: Jeroen Musch

The 100 Resilient Cities programme is being wound down, but its fundamental ethos of breaking down silos and combining budgets has transformed the way some cities spend their money, including Rotterdam. Instead of a pot for road maintenance, there might be a pot for more liveable streets, and the money is spent on anything that contributes to a top-line vision of what they would like to achieve.

Van Peijpe says resilient thinking has even led to schools upgrading city drainage systems as part of playground projects: "They can provide children with greener playgrounds while installing rainwater collection."

I ask van Peijpe what he has learned in the five years since the opening of his water square, and he reveals that his thinking has shifted dramatically.

He says: "Fundamentally, we took a drainage approach – we drained the water, even if it didn't go into the sewer. We now want to move away from drainage completely, to keep the water in the square, either in the soil or some kind of aquifer.

"We need to move from being a drainage city to a sponge city."

He adds that China is working on a massive programme along these lines.

"We want to keep the water in the city and be able to bring it back when we need

it. Climate adaptation and resilience is about dealing with extremes – too much water or too little. Through soil with sponge conditions, such as peat, clay or rubble, and certain plantings, or even by replenishing aquifers, we can absorb excess water but get it back during droughts."

Pilot sites are viewed as critical to testing De Urbanisten's ideas and near its office, it is now experimenting with a sponge garden. The firm recently tweeted how impressed it has been with the garden's resistance to drought.

Another shift for van Peijpe is the move to 'depave' our cities. Both an activist movement and design approach, depaving involves literally digging up the pavement or asphalt to create more permeable, greener streets.

He says: "The reality is that most public spaces are designed not by landscape architects or other architects, but by traffic engineers."

Depaving takes a street-by-street approach. Van Peijpe explains: "You look at how much paving you actually need, for vehicles, parking and so-on. Then you remove as much as possible to incorporate plantings, rainwater or infiltration tanks."

This should make the streets more resilient, and more attractive, he argues, and depaving can be incorporated into road improvement plans.

"Instead of just maintaining roads, with the same money you can make the city more resilient," he says.

But van Peijpe admits that changing the mindset of traffic engineers and road maintenance crews is necessary. Test projects can help with this – but he says they are also considering publishing guidance.

Overall, he is optimistic about its widespread adoption. "Depaving is already going on in the first metre outside people's houses, where they are planting it themselves."

On a recent trip to Paris, van Peijpe was also impressed by community gardens sprouting around the base of city trees. He says: "These explosions of wildflowers are a radical departure from formal French gardening. It shows me that an appreciation is growing for a different sort of green. These ecosystems provide more than functional drainage value as well, such as flora and fauna, contributing to active healthy living and they raise the value of the real estate, too.

"Cities are more and more considered attractive places where people want to stay. People who really want to stay also want to take care of their front yard. We have a more active population, and people are involved in making their own environment greener and softer. It's low-maintenance, lush and green, and the community is looking after it."

People are leaving London due to air pollution: we are the problem

As developers march in the Climate Strike and London has its biggest car-free day, Anna White reports on the pressing need for the development industry to clean up its act. With reporting by Christine Murray from the Climate Strike

Stretched affordability and the quest for more space are not the only reason people are leaving London in record numbers for suburbs, smaller towns and villages. The air pollution public health crisis is another.

In 2017, two out of three Londoners said in a survey by AnyVan.com they would quit the city to escape its toxic air. Figures released by the Office for National Statistics (ONS) revealed 340,500 people moved out of the capital in the 12 months before June 2018, the largest number ever recorded since the ONS began collecting data in 2012.

London's toxic atmosphere costs the economy £3.7bn a year and a quarter of the capital's primary schools are in neighbourhoods that breach the legal limit for poisonous nitrogen oxides (NO_x). The busiest roads glow an ominous red on the city's air quality maps due to dangerous particles emitted by diesel vehicles, PM_{10} and PM_{25}, and nitrogen dioxide (NO_2).

The boroughs with the dirtiest air, according to a study by Arup, are Westminster, Hillingdon, Tower Hamlets, Ealing and Barnet. However, Lewisham is in the spotlight, with a second inquest under way into the tragic death of nine-year-old Ella Kissi-Debrah. This fresh investigation followed a report last year that linked her fatal asthma attack in 2013 to air pollution. She lived by the South Circular in Lewisham where NO_2 is at illegal highs.

But escaping the city centre for cleaner air is not necessarily the answer – and for many who need to be close to work or family, leaving is not an option.

Living by a busy through-road in a leafy suburb could be worse than standing in the middle of Hyde Park. It is about proximity to cars and combustion. A child inside a car on the daily school run is more exposed to fumes than a cyclist speeding down Piccadilly. A blazing log burner (wherever you live) is the equivalent of a 7.5-tonne diesel lorry idling in the driveway.

"Where there are humans there is air pollution," says sustainability author Tim Smedley, whose book, *Clearing the Air*, was shortlisted for the Royal Society of Science Book Prize 2019.

While the problem is much magnified in an urban environment at the moment, Smedley believes solutions will come to cities much sooner than to towns and villages where public transport infrastructure is archaic.

Slowly but surely, London is cleaning up its act by reversing its reliance on the car, but lags behind other global cities.

The centre of Oslo is completely car-free and China is the world leader in electric vehicles. Shenzhen transport, for example, is 100% electric with 19,000 e-buses and 20,000 e-taxis.

Historically cloaked in smog, Los Angeles has the best clean air laws in the world, according to Smedley. Fuel nozzles are covered in a plastic sheath so no particles leak into the atmosphere when at the pump. "When Europe went gung-ho for diesel cars (the science said they emit less CO_2 than petrol cars), LA was focused on the electric car and now has a high ownership rate," he explains.

The current mayor of London is going in the right direction. In September, Sadiq Khan announced that two of London's bus routes are becoming exclusively electric. London has more than 200 e-buses, making it Europe's largest fleet. This will continue to grow next year, as Transport for London (TfL) has awarded contracts to operators for a further 78 e-double-deckers, which will carry around 18.5 million passengers across the capital each year.

Double-decker hydrogen-powered buses that only emit water are also on the way and in Southampton, after a successful pilot, the Go-Ahead Group is expanding its fleet of buses that suck pollutants out of the air.

It is not just moving vehicles in London that are the problem – 2.7 million privately owner parked cars take up £172bn of land.

There are 868 car parks in London within a mile of a train or tube station, 400 of which are owned by local authorities and on which 80,000 new homes could be built, research by property group JLL reveals.

Nick Whitten, author of the study *The Direction of Travel for Automotive Real Estate*, suggests that privately-owned diesel or petrol cars should be phased out of city centres and the roads put to a cleaner use.

Rather than a network of unhealthy arteries clogged up with traffic, Whitten's sketch of the future cityscape has roads replaced with wider cycle lanes, linear parks, canals and tree trenches (long sunken beds for trees and foliage that absorb excess rainwater while naturally filtering the air).

His vision is littered with living walls, CO_2 absorption plants, smart bike storage and chargers for electric cars. Whitten foresees e-bus fleets that change route depending on where wannabe passengers are waiting and electric car sharing schemes "a bit like shared Uber on-demand".

What is better than electric cars? No cars. E-vehicles do not emit exhaust fumes but they still produce large amounts of tiny pollution particles from brake and tyre dust, for which the government already accepts there is no safe limit. "Fewer cars, not cleaner cars are the answer," says government advisor Professor Frank Kelly.

London's toxic atmosphere costs the economy £3.7bn a year

Cars are not the only contributing factor to the air quality crisis, however. "The built environment is responsible for 37% of nitrogen oxide emissions," says energy and sustainability expert Barny Evans, technical director at engineering firm WSP.

If Whitten is advocating turning over space taken up by parked cars to house builders, construction must get cleaner, too. There have been improvements in the industry, explains Gary Fuller, author of *The Invisible Killer: the Rising Global Threat of Air Pollution – and How We Can Fight Back*. He is leading a working party between the Mayor's Office, King's College and councils including Camden, Islington and Lambeth to lower emissions from the construction industry. "We no longer use wrecking balls to demolish buildings. Machinery that nibbles away at the concrete, reducing dust significantly, is now used," he says.

Smedley cites Delhi as one of the worst cities he has visited for unregulated and polluting construction sites. "Uncovered piles of cement and sand would blow across the streets killing street dogs and waste burnt in the open," he says.

The overlap between traffic and construction is an overlooked yet dangerous part of the build process. Harmful particles (PM_{10} – the number defines the size of particle) are dropped along roads as lorries transport building waste.

Architect Rory Bergin of HTA Design says old construction trucks themselves are a major contributor to air pollution.

"The Ultra Low Emission Zones (ULEZs) should force firms to update their vehicles," he adds. Surely ULEZs should therefore be rolled out across all UK cities.

Typically preoccupied with the promotion of their schemes as either 'affordable' or 'luxury', when they may be neither, developers are starting to shout about their green credentials.

Canary Wharf Group's new 345-unit residential tower 10 Park Drive is the first construction site to support the mayor of

It's all about proximity to cars and combustion. A child inside a car on the daily school run is more exposed to fumes than a cyclist speeding down Piccadilly. A blazing log burner (wherever you live) is the equivalent of a 7.5-tonne diesel lorry idling in the driveway

London's Clean Air campaign, badged a Considerate Constructors Scheme ultra site. Lorry drivers must turn idling engines off and 'healthy' building materials are being used, including water-based paint – the industry has moved away from oil-based, which gives off particles even when dry.

Materials are critical to low-carbon construction. The new buzzword is whole-life carbon, taking into account everything from the CO_2 from making the bricks and shipping them to site (embodied carbon) to the emissions from the building in use.

Tracing the environmental impact of every material is something architect Peter Clegg, partner at Feilden Clegg Bradley Studios, did 30 years ago, when designing Greenpeace's headquarters. "That's why we went with timber windows, even though at the time the slogan was 'save a tree, use PVC'.

"Now we use a lot of PVC in our buildings. We need to find out about how our materials are sourced, what the recycling provision is and reduce usage."

The architecture firm recently made its office canteen vegetarian and audited its rubbish to reduce its carbon footprint. The practice worked out that every vegan lunch offsets the office's daily train and paper usage. But Clegg, who is on the steering committee of Architects' Declare, a campaign that has seen more than 600 practices sign a pledge to pursue low-carbon architecture, knows the biggest impact the practice can have is through its buildings, by designing out things like concrete and steel.

Nick Searl, partner at developer Argent, agrees. He, alongside Clegg and hundreds of other built environment professionals, marched to Millbank for the Climate Strike on 20 September. "It's clear that we need to be focusing on embodied carbon, not just operational," says Searl. "I've heard that can account for up to 60% of a building's carbon emissions."

Searl believes the industry is waking up and willing to take action. "For the first time, we are on the cusp of real change. We're having a lot more meaningful conversations."

He adds: "What's driving the change is this," pointing at the thousands of adult and pupil protestors on the streets. "It's public perception, from tenants to the wider movement, and most importantly perhaps, a new mood."

Searl also says pension funds and larger investors are demanding greener buildings, which is driving change. "It's not altruism. They see value in doing the right thing. There's a fundamental shift to longer-term thinking."

As for the Circular Economy, which would involve reusing materials in construction, such as bricks or aggregate, Searl believes it is "on the horizon". He says: "I went to a big meeting at the [Greater London Authority] looking at how the Circular Economy can be built into policy."

Bergin claims cleaner construction means manufacturing prefabricated homes offsite in factories. This halves activities on open sites, often in residential or built-up areas. "In a factory, everything is contained and dust is dealt with by vacuum machines," he says.

Pre-fab off-site construction is still the exception, not the rule, in a sector that is under pressure to deliver homes fast but is also slow to change. "There is inertia in this conservative industry, the rationale being that a construction project failure is very expensive. Due to tight margins, developers also put very little investment into research and development," says Bergin.

The use of timber creates a healthier working environment during its construction and makes the build process faster, thereby reducing environmental impact.

Green roofs and wild flowers are being planted to attract species and pollinators. Greening and rewilding of the urban scape is another way the developers can reduce air pollution – even if it is sometimes a planning condition rather than a proactive eco-innovation.

At Westgate House in Brentford, 83 homes have been built right next to the M4 corridor. The challenge was to design a scheme that would reduce the toxicity of the air in and around the development. A 10-floor internal living wall, Europe's biggest, helps to clean the air.

Architecture practice Assael worked with landscape architects Fabrik to design the living green wall, one of Europe's largest at 10 storeys, in the atrium and a twin-skin glazed facade with a gap of 1.5 metres between the two layers.

"This acts as a natural chimney for the

Westgate House has a 10-storey green wall

Families on the South Circular demanding Lewisham Council reduce air pollution. Photo: Alamy

outside air to rise and helps control the internal temperature of the atrium," says Assael's Russell Pedley.

Air filters on the roof sift the air and cut NO_x levels by 40%. This air is then driven into the atrium, where it is cleaned again by the plants. The air is then finally pumped into homes.

All schemes by the developer HUB have mechanical ventilation and heat recovery systems, aka MVHR, which prevent heat leaking out into the atmosphere while allowing stale air to be extracted from the homes and fresher external air to be drawn in. They also take out any major air pollutants.

MVHR is becoming more commonplace in new builds but Bergin is sceptical. "These systems are getting more complicated and there is no proof they are being correctly installed – we don't know what we're doing is working," he says.

What is the point anyway, if you step outside your air-filtered home into an air quality blackspot? Back in Lewisham, where Ella Kissi-Debrah died, planning was controversially granted for a residential scheme by Bluecroft Property Development right next to the A2. An air quality assessment showed the site contained 56.3µg of NO_2 per cubic metre where the legal maximum is 40µg. The strategic planning

Ella Kissi-Debrah died from air pollution

committee report requires the developer to advise residents to keep their windows closed and pay £7,500 towards monitoring air quality.

"Here's the good news – we have the solutions to air pollution," says Smedley. "Unlike climate change there is no 2º scenario, no knowledge that suggests things are going to get worse whatever we do. Urban air pollution is local, short-lived, and can be stopped at the source."

Even more good news is the opportunity for developers to make a huge impact. According to Ben Smallwood from engineer Buro Happold, every 1% reduction in carbon emissions on the Temple Quarter project in Bristol is equivalent to 250 people going vegan for life. "You can make a huge difference," he told an audience of architects

at Feilden Clegg Bradley Studios.

An update from the London Atmospheric Emission Inventory earlier this year suggested NO_x levels are falling and could reach legal levels within six years.

Perhaps at this point there will be a stampede back into the capital in pursuit of Whitten's urban idyll.

In the photobooth:
Essex

Marco Ferrari coaxes
passers-by into a
photobooth in the Intu
Lakeside shopping mall in
Essex, where they reveal
their likes and dislikes
of the mall, their home
towns and the county

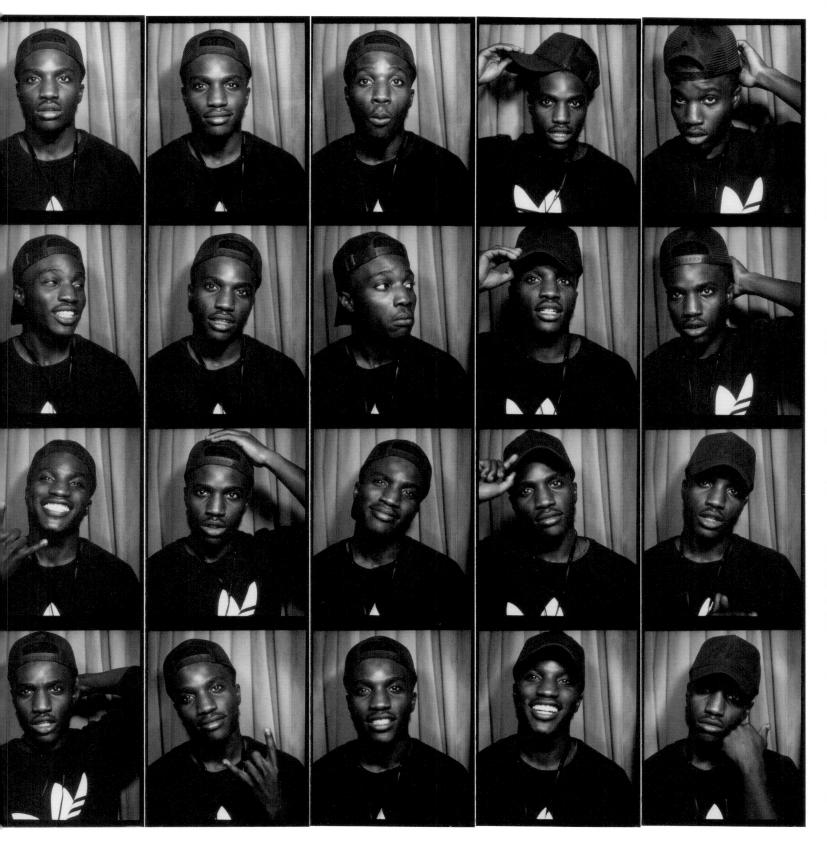

In the photobooth Daniel, 19, from Rainham **What do you like about your home town?** I like how relaxed, how friendly it is, compared to a bigger town. I used to work at the corner store and all the customers that came in were very friendly people and you could get to know them by name, know their family. It's a nice area to be in – everyone cares **What would you change?** I would change some people's attitude. There is some violence, gang activity, drugs. People carry knives. In terms of buildings and planning, there is sometimes a lack of maintenance of green spaces. Walking down my road, I have to duck under some trees – it's not a big deal, but some care would help

In the photobooth Jeremy, 49, from Hornchurch **What do you like about your home town?** It's a good location to get into London or to the coast. I was born near here but I lived in London for 15 years. I came back to Essex with my children because it's a good area for them to grow up **What would you change?** I would turn it into something like Margate or Brighton. Put a lot of sand on one side and a lot of water. Jokes apart, there is a lot to be done to revitalise the area

In the photobooth Olivia, 18, from Westcliff-on-Sea **Why are you eating here?** There is so much more on offer here. The food isn't very nice in Westcliff. **What do you like about your home town?** I like that in Westcliff, when the sun is out, you can go to the beach and sunbathe. **What would you change?** I don't like it when people leave their rubbish at the beach. There's a lot of pollution – it's not right and it looks dirty

In the photobooth Sam, 18, from Southend **Why are you shopping here and not online?** You can see different shops, try things on and compare them **What do you like about your home town?** You have the seaside but also rural areas so you can easily go to the countryside. At the same time, it's quite busy in the town so it's a nice mix **What would you change?** Nothing really about the city. It's just that there is quite a lot of crime – I feel it's getting worse

In the photobooth Louise, 18, from Southend **Why are you shopping here and not online?** I prefer to see the clothes in person and browse through them **What do you like about your home town?** The seaside **What would you change?** Nothing about the city itself, but the people sometimes, their mentality